KURT VONNEGUT

KURT VONNEGUT
THE LAST INTERVIEW
and OTHER CONVERSATIONS

edited by TOM McCARTAN

MELVILLE HOUSE
BROOKLYN, NEW YORK

KURT VONNEGUT: THE LAST INTERVIEW

Melville House Publishing
145 Plymouth Street
Brooklyn, NY 11201

www.mhpbooks.com

ISBN: 978-1-61219-090-7

Printed in the United States of America

A catalog record for this book is available from the Library of Congress

CONTENTS

EDITOR'S NOTE

The last interview referred to in the title of this volume is in fact Kurt Vonnegut's last published conversation, an interview conducted on February 28, 2007, by Heather Augustyn and published online May 9, 2007, by *In These Times* magazine, where Vonnegut himself often wrote. Also included here is J. Rentilly's June 2007 *U.S. Airways Magazine* interview, which contains quotes from a conversation between Rentilly and Vonnegut that came after Augustyn's interview. Rentilly's interview draws on four conversations he had with Vonnegut between October 2000 and March 6, 2007, one month before Vonnegut's passing at age 84.

KURT VONNEGUT, THE ART OF FICTION

INTERVIEWED BY DAVID HAYMAN, DAVID MICHAELIS, GEORGE PLIMPTON, RICHARD RHODES

FIRST PUBLISHED IN *THE PARIS REVIEW* NO. 69, SPRING 1977

This interview with Kurt Vonnegut was originally a composite of four interviews done with the author over the past decade. The composite has gone through an extensive working over by the subject himself, who looks upon his own spoken words on the page with considerable misgiving . . . indeed, what follows can be considered an interview conducted with himself, by himself.

The introduction to the first of the incorporated interviews (done in West Barnstable, Massachusetts, when Vonnegut was forty-four) reads: "He is a veteran and a family man, large-boned, loose-jointed, at ease. He camps in an armchair in a shaggy tweed jacket, Cambridge gray flannels, a blue Brooks Brothers shirt, slouched down, his hands stuffed into his pockets. He shells the interview with explosive coughs and sneezes, windages of an autumn cold and a lifetime of heavy cigarette smoking. His voice is a resonant baritone, Midwestern, wry in its inflections. From time to time he issues the open, alert smile of a man who has seen and reserved within himself almost everything: depression, war, the possibility of violent death, the inanities of corporate public relations, six children, an irregular income, long-delayed recognition."

The last of the interviews that made up the composite

was conducted during the summer of 1976, years after the first. The description of him at this time reads: "...he moves with the low-keyed amiability of an old family dog. In general, his appearance is tousled: the long curly hair, mustache, and sympathetic smile suggest a man at once amused and saddened by the world around him. He has rented the Gerald Murphy house for the summer. He works in the little bedroom at the end of a hall where Murphy, artist, bon vivant, and friend to the artistic great, died in 1964. From his desk Vonnegut can look out onto the front lawn through a small window; behind him is a large, white canopy bed. On the desk next to the typewriter is a copy of Andy Warhol's *Interview*, Clancy Sigal's *Zone of the Interior*, and several discarded cigarette packs.

"Vonnegut has chain-smoked Pall Malls since 1936 and during the course of the interview he smokes the better part of one pack. His voice is low and gravelly, and as he speaks, the incessant procedure of lighting the cigarettes and exhaling smoke is like punctuation in his conversation. Other distractions, such as the jangle of the telephone and the barking of a small, shaggy dog named Pumpkin, do not detract from Vonnegut's good-natured disposition. Indeed, as Dan Wakefield once said of his fellow Shortridge High School alumnus, 'He laughed a lot and was kind to everyone.'"

INTERVIEWER

You are a veteran of the Second World War?

VONNEGUT

Yes. I want a military funeral when I die—the bugler, the flag on the casket, the ceremonial firing squad, the hallowed ground.

INTERVIEWER

Why?

VONNEGUT

It will be a way of achieving what I've always wanted more than anything—something I could have had, if only I'd managed to get myself killed in the war.

INTERVIEWER

Which is—?

VONNEGUT

The unqualified approval of my community.

INTERVIEWER

You don't feel that you have that now?

VONNEGUT

My relatives say that they are glad I'm rich, but that they simply cannot read me.

INTERVIEWER

You were an infantry battalion scout in the war?

VONNEGUT

Yes, but I took my basic training on the 240-millimeter
howitzer.

INTERVIEWER

A rather large weapon.

VONNEGUT

The largest mobile fieldpiece in the army at that time. This
weapon came in six pieces, each piece dragged wallow-
ingly by a Caterpillar tractor. Whenever we were told to
fire it, we had to build it first. We practically had to invent
it. We lowered one piece on top of another, using cranes
and jacks. The shell itself was about nine and a half inches
in diameter and weighed three hundred pounds. We con-
structed a miniature railway which would allow us to deliver the shell from the ground to the breech, which was
about eight feet above grade. The breechblock was like the
door on the vault of a savings and loan association in Peru,
Indiana, say.

INTERVIEWER

It must have been a thrill to fire such a weapon.

VONNEGUT

Not really. We would put the shell in there, and then we
would throw in bags of very slow and patient explosives.
They were damp dog biscuits, I think. We would close the
breech, and then trip a hammer which hit a fulminate of

mercury percussion cap, which spit fire at the damp dog biscuits. The main idea, I think, was to generate steam. After a while, we could hear these cooking sounds. It was a lot like cooking a turkey. In utter safety, I think, we could have opened the breechblock from time to time, and basted the shell. Eventually, though, the howitzer always got restless. And finally it would heave back on its recoil mechanism, and it would have to expectorate the shell. The shell would come floating out like the Goodyear blimp. If we had had a stepladder, we could have painted "Fuck Hitler" on the shell as it left the gun. Helicopters could have taken after it and shot it down.

INTERVIEWER

The ultimate terror weapon.

VONNEGUT

Of the Franco-Prussian War.

INTERVIEWER

But you were ultimately sent overseas not with this instrument but with the 106th Infantry Division—

VONNEGUT

"The Bag Lunch Division." They used to feed us a lot of bag lunches. Salami sandwiches. An orange.

INTERVIEWER

In combat?

VONNEGUT

When we were still in the States.

INTERVIEWER

While they trained you for the infantry?

VONNEGUT

I was never trained for the infantry. Battalion scouts were elite troops, see. There were only six in each battalion, and nobody was very sure about what they were supposed to do. So we would march over to the rec room every morning, and play Ping-Pong and fill out applications for Officer Candidate School.

INTERVIEWER

During your basic training, though, you must have been familiarized with weapons other than the howitzer.

VONNEGUT

If you study the 240-millimeter howitzer, you don't even have time left over for a venereal-disease film.

INTERVIEWER

What happened when you reached the front?

VONNEGUT

I imitated various war movies I'd seen.

INTERVIEWER

Did you shoot anybody in the war?

VONNEGUT

I thought about it. I did fix my bayonet once, fully expecting to charge.

INTERVIEWER

Did you charge?

VONNEGUT

No. If everybody else had charged, I would have charged, too. But we decided not to charge. We couldn't see anybody.

INTERVIEWER

This was during the Battle of the Bulge, wasn't it? It was the largest defeat of American arms in history.

VONNEGUT

Probably. My last mission as a scout was to find our own artillery. Usually, scouts go out and look for enemy stuff. Things got so bad that we were finally looking for our own stuff. If I'd found our own battalion commander, everybody would have thought that was pretty swell.

INTERVIEWER

Do you mind describing your capture by the Germans?

VONNEGUT

Gladly. We were in this gully about as deep as a World War I trench. There was snow all around. Somebody said we were probably in Luxembourg. We were out of food.

INTERVIEWER

Who was "we"?

VONNEGUT

Our battalion scouting unit. All six of us. And about fifty people we'd never met before. The Germans could see us, because they were talking to us through a loudspeaker. They told us our situation was hopeless, and so on. That was when we fixed bayonets. It was nice there for a few minutes.

INTERVIEWER

How so?

VONNEGUT

Being a porcupine with all those steel quills. I pitied any-body who had to come in after us.

INTERVIEWER

But they came in anyway?

VONNEGUT

No. They sent in eighty-eight millimeter shells instead. The shells burst in the treetops right over us. Those were very loud bangs right over our heads. We were showered with splintered steel. Some people got hit. Then the Germans told us again to come out. We didn't yell "Nuts" or anything like that. We said, "Okay," and "Take it easy," and so on. When the Germans finally showed themselves, we saw they were wearing white camouflage suits. We didn't have anything like that. We were olive drab. No matter what season it was, we were olive drab.

INTERVIEWER

What did the Germans say?

VONNEGUT

They said the war was all over for us, that we were lucky, that we could now be sure we would live through the war, which was more than they could be sure of. As a matter of fact, they were probably killed or captured by Patton's Third Army within the next few days. Wheels within wheels.

INTERVIEWER

Did you speak any German?

VONNEGUT

I had heard my parents speak it a lot. They hadn't taught me how to do it, since there had been such bitterness in America against all things German during the First World War. I tried a few words I knew on our captors, and they asked me if I was of German ancestry, and I said, "Yes." They wanted to know why I was making war against my brothers.

INTERVIEWER

And you said—?

VONNEGUT

I honestly found the question ignorant and comical. My parents had separated me so thoroughly from my Germanic past that my captors might as well have been Bolivians or Tibetans, for all they meant to me.

INTERVIEWER

After you were captured, you were shipped to Dresden?

VONNEGUT

In the same boxcars that had brought up the troops that captured us—probably in the same boxcars that had delivered Jews and Gypsies and Jehovah's Witnesses and so on to the extermination camps. Rolling stock is rolling stock. British Mosquito bombers attacked us at night a few times. I guess they thought we were strategic materials of some kind. They hit a car containing most of the officers from our battalion. Every time I say I hate officers, which I still do fairly frequently, I have to remind myself that practically none of the officers I served under survived. Christmas was in there somewhere.

INTERVIEWER

And you finally arrived in Dresden.

VONNEGUT

In a huge prison camp south of Dresden first. The privates were separated from the noncoms and officers. Under the articles of the Geneva Convention, which is a very Edwardian document, privates were required to work for their keep. Everybody else got to languish in prison. As a private, I was shipped to Dresden...

INTERVIEWER

What were your impressions of the city itself before the bombing?

VONNEGUT

The first fancy city I'd ever seen. A city full of statues and zoos, like Paris. We were living in a slaughterhouse, in a nice new cement-block hog barn. They put bunks and straw mattresses in the barn, and we went to work every morning as contract labor in a malt-syrup factory. The syrup was for pregnant women. The damned sirens would go off and we'd hear some other city getting it—*whump a whump a whumpa whump*. We never expected to get it. There were very few air-raid shelters in town and no war industries, just cigarette factories, hospitals, clarinet factories. Then a siren went off—it was February 13, 1945—and we went down two stories under the pavement into a big meat locker. It was cool there, with cadavers hanging all around. When we came up the city was gone.

INTERVIEWER

You didn't suffocate in the meat locker?

VONNEGUT

No. It was quite large, and there weren't very many of us.
The attack didn't sound like a hell of a lot either. *Whump*.
They went over with high explosives first to loosen things
up, and then scattered incendiaries. When the war started,
incendiaries were fairly sizable, about as long as a shoebox.
By the time Dresden got it, they were tiny little things. They
burnt the whole damn town down.

INTERVIEWER

What happened when you came up?

VONNEGUT

Our guards were noncoms—a sergeant, a corporal, and
four privates—and leaderless. Cityless, too, because they
were Dresdeners who'd been shot up on the front and sent
home for easy duty. They kept us at attention for a couple of hours. They didn't know what else to do. They'd go
over and talk to each other. Finally we trekked across the
rubble and they quartered us with some South Africans in
a suburb. Every day we walked into the city and dug into
basements and shelters to get the corpses out, as a sanitary
measure. When we went into them, a typical shelter, an
ordinary basement usually, looked like a streetcar full of
people who'd simultaneously had heart failure. Just people sitting there in their chairs, all dead. A firestorm is an

amazing thing. It doesn't occur in nature. It's fed by the tornadoes that occur in the midst of it and there isn't a damned thing to breathe. We brought the dead out. They were loaded on wagons and taken to parks, large, open areas in the city which weren't filled with rubble. The Germans got funeral pyres going, burning the bodies to keep them from stinking and from spreading disease. One hundred thirty thousand corpses were hidden underground. It was a terribly elaborate Easter-egg hunt. We went to work through cordons of German soldiers. Civilians didn't get to see what we were up to. After a few days the city began to smell, and a new technique was invented. Necessity is the mother of invention. We would bust into the shelter, gather up valuables from people's laps without attempting identification, and turn the valuables over to guards. Then soldiers would come in with a flamethrower and stand in the door and cremate the people inside. Get the gold and jewelry out and then burn everybody inside.

INTERVIEWER

What an impression on someone thinking of becoming a writer!

VONNEGUT

It was a fancy thing to see, a startling thing. It was a moment of truth, too, because American civilians and ground troops didn't know American bombers were engaged in saturation bombing. It was kept a secret until very close to the end of the war. One reason they burned down Dresden is that they'd already burned down everything else. You know: "What're we going to do tonight?" Here was everybody all set to go, and Germany still fighting, and this machinery for burning down cities was being used. It was a secret, burning down cities—boiling pisspots and flaming prams. There was all this hokum about the Norden bomb sight. You'd see a newsreel showing a bombardier with an MP on either side of him holding a drawn .45. That sort of nonsense, and hell, all they were doing was just flying over cities, hundreds of airplanes, and dropping everything. When I went to the University of Chicago after the war the guy who interviewed me for admission had bombed Dresden. He got to that part of my life story and he said, "Well, we hated to do it." The comment sticks in my mind.

INTERVIEWER

Another reaction would be, "We were ordered to do it."

VONNEGUT

His was more humane. I think he felt the bombing was necessary, and it may have been. One thing everybody learned is how fast you can rebuild a city. The engineers said it would take five hundred years to rebuild Germany. Actually it took about eighteen weeks.

INTERVIEWER

Did you intend to write about it as soon as you went through the experience?

VONNEGUT

When the city was demolished I had no idea of the scale of the thing ... Whether this was what Bremen looked like or Hamburg, Coventry ... I'd never seen Coventry, so I had no scale except for what I'd seen in movies. When I got home (I was a writer since I had been on the *Cornell Sun,* except that was the extent of my writing) I thought of writing my war story, too. All my friends were home; they'd had wonderful adventures, too. I went down to the newspaper office, the *Indianapolis News,* and looked to find out what they had about Dresden. There was an item about half an inch long, which said our planes had been over Dresden and two had been lost. And so I figured, well, this really was the most minor sort of detail in World War II. Others had so much more to write about. I remember envying Andy Rooney, who jumped into print at that time; I didn't know him, but I think he was the first guy to publish his war story after the war; it was called *Air Gunner*. Hell, I never had any classy adventure like that. But every so often I would meet a European and we would be talking about the war and I would say I was in Dresden; he'd be astonished that I'd been there, and he'd always want to know more. Then a book by David Irving was published about Dresden, saying it was the largest massacre in European history. I said, By God, I saw something after all! I would try to write my war story, whether it was interesting or not, and try to make something out of it. I describe that process a little in the beginning of *Slaughterhouse-Five;* I saw it as starring John Wayne and Frank Sinatra. Finally, a girl called Mary O'Hare, the wife of a friend of mine who'd been there with me, said, "You were just children then. It's not fair to pretend that you were men like Wayne and Sinatra, and it's not fair to future generations, because you're going to make war look good." That was a very important clue to me.

INTERVIEWER

That sort of shifted the whole focus . . .

VONNEGUT

She freed me to write about what infants we really were: seventeen, eighteen, nineteen, twenty, twenty-one. We were baby-faced, and as a prisoner of war I don't think I had to shave very often. I don't recall that that was a problem.

INTERVIEWER

One more war question: Do you still think about the fire-bombing of Dresden at all?

VONNEGUT

I wrote a book about it, called *Slaughterhouse-Five*. The book is still in print, and I have to do something about it as a businessman now and then. Marcel Ophuls asked me to be in his film, *The Memory of Justice*. He wanted me to talk about Dresden as an atrocity. I told him to talk to my friend Bernard V. O'Hare, Mary's husband, instead, which he did. O'Hare was a fellow battalion scout, and then a fellow prisoner of war. He's a lawyer in Pennsylvania now.

INTERVIEWER

Why didn't you wish to testify?

VONNEGUT

I had a German name. I didn't want to argue with people who thought Dresden should have been bombed to hell. All I ever said in my book was that Dresden, willy-nilly, *was* bombed to hell.

INTERVIEWER

It was the largest massacre in European history?

VONNEGUT

It was the fastest killing of large numbers of people—one hundred and thirty-five thousand people in a matter of hours. There were slower schemes for killing, of course.

INTERVIEWER

The death camps.

VONNEGUT

Yes—in which millions were eventually killed. Many people see the Dresden massacre as correct and quite minimal revenge for what had been done by the camps. Maybe so. As I say, I never argue that point. I do note in passing that the death penalty was applied to absolutely anybody who happened to be in the undefended city—babies, old people, the zoo animals, and thousands upon thousands of rabid Nazis, of course, and, among others, my best friend

Bernard V. O'Hare and me. By all rights, O'Hare and I should have been part of the body count. The more bodies, the more correct the revenge.

INTERVIEWER

The Franklin Library is bringing out a deluxe edition of *Slaughterhouse-Five,* I believe.

VONNEGUT

Yes. I was required to write a new introduction for it.

INTERVIEWER

Did you have any new thoughts?

VONNEGUT

I said that only one person on the entire planet benefited from the raid, which must have cost tens of millions of dollars. The raid didn't shorten the war by half a second, didn't weaken a German defense or attack anywhere, didn't free a single person from a death camp. Only one person benefited—not two or five or ten. Just one.

INTERVIEWER

And who was that?

VONNEGUT

Me. I got three dollars for each person killed. Imagine that.

INTERVIEWER

How much affinity do you feel toward your contemporaries?

VONNEGUT

My brother and sister writers? Friendly, certainly. It's hard for me to talk to some of them, since we seem to be in very different sorts of businesses. This was a mystery to me for a while, but then Saul Steinberg—

INTERVIEWER

The graphic artist?

VONNEGUT

Indeed. He said that in almost all arts, there were some people who responded strongly to art history, to triumphs and fiascoes and experiments of the past, and others who did not. I fell into the second group, and had to. I couldn't play games with my literary ancestors, since I had never studied them systematically. My education was as a chemist at Cornell and then an anthropologist at the University of Chicago. Christ—I was thirty-five before I went crazy about Blake, forty before I read *Madame Bovary*, forty-five before I'd even heard of Céline. Through dumb luck, I read *Look Homeward, Angel* exactly when I was supposed to.

INTERVIEWER

When?

VONNEGUT

At the age of eighteen.

INTERVIEWER

So you've always been a reader?

VONNEGUT

Yes. I grew up in a house crammed with books. But I never had to read a book for academic credit, never had to write a paper about it, never had to prove I'd understood it in a seminar. I am a hopelessly clumsy discusser of books. My experience is nil.

INTERVIEWER

Which member of your family had the most influence on you as a writer?

VONNEGUT

My mother, I guess. Edith Lieber Vonnegut. After our family lost almost all of its money in the Great Depression, my mother thought she might make a new fortune by writing for the slick magazines. She took short-story courses at night. She studied magazines the way gamblers study racing forms.

INTERVIEWER

She'd been rich at one time?

VONNEGUT

My father, an architect of modest means, married one of
the richest girls in town. It was a brewing fortune based on
Lieber Lager Beer and then Gold Medal Beer. Lieber Lager
became Gold Medal after winning a prize at some Paris
exposition.

INTERVIEWER

It must have been a very good beer.

VONNEGUT

Long before my time. I never tasted any. It had a secret
ingredient, I know. My grandfather and his brewmaster
wouldn't let anybody watch while they put it in.

INTERVIEWER

Do you know what it was?

VONNEGUT

Coffee.

INTERVIEWER

So your mother studied short-story writing—

VONNEGUT

And my father painted pictures in a studio he'd set up on
the top floor of the house. There wasn't much work for
architects during the Great Depression—not much work
for anybody. Strangely enough, though, Mother was right:

Even mediocre magazine writers were making money hand over fist.

So your mother took a very practical attitude toward writing.

Not to say crass. She was a highly intelligent, cultivated woman, by the way. She went to the same high school I did, and was one of the few people who got nothing but A-pluses while she was there. She went east to a finishing school after that, and then traveled all over Europe. She was fluent in German and French. I still have her high-school report cards somewhere. "A-plus, A-plus, A-plus..." She was a good writer, it turned out, but she had no talent for the vulgarity the slick magazines required. Fortunately, I was loaded with vulgarity, so, when I grew up, I was able to make her dream come true. Writing for *Collier's* and *The Saturday Evening Post* and *Cosmopolitan* and *Ladies' Home Journal* and so on was as easy as falling off a log for me. I only wish she'd lived to see it. I only wish she'd lived to see all her grandchildren. She has ten. She didn't even get to see the first one. I made another one of her dreams come true: I lived on Cape Cod for many years. She always wanted to live on Cape Cod. It's probably very common for sons to try to make their mothers' impossible dreams come true. I adopted my sister's sons after she died, and it's spooky to watch them try to make her impossible dreams come true.

INTERVIEWER

What were your sister's dreams like?

VONNEGUT

She wanted to live like a member of *The Swiss Family Robinson,* with impossibly friendly animals in impossibly congenial isolation. Her oldest son, Jim, has been a goat farmer on a mountaintop in Jamaica for the past eight years. No telephone. No electricity.

INTERVIEWER

The Indianapolis high school you and your mother attended—

VONNEGUT

And my father. Shortridge High.

INTERVIEWER

It had a daily paper, I believe.

VONNEGUT

Yes. *The Shortridge Daily Echo.* There was a print shop right in the school. Students wrote the paper. Students set the type. After school.

INTERVIEWER

You just laughed about something.

VONNEGUT

It was something dumb I remembered about high school. It doesn't have anything to do with writing.

INTERVIEWER

You care to share it with us anyway?

VONNEGUT

Oh—I just remembered something that happened in a high-school course on civics, on how our government worked. The teacher asked each of us to stand up in turn and tell what we did after school. I was sitting in the back of the room, sitting next to a guy named J. T. Alburger. He later became an insurance man in Los Angeles. He died fairly recently. Anyway—he kept nudging me, urging me, daring me to tell the truth about what I did after school. He offered me five dollars to tell the truth. He wanted me to stand up and say, "I make model airplanes and jerk off."

INTERVIEWER

I see.

VONNEGUT

I also worked on *The Shortridge Daily Echo*.

INTERVIEWER

Was that fun?

VONNEGUT

Fun and easy. I've always found it easy to write. Also, I learned to write for peers rather than for teachers. Most beginning writers don't get to write for peers—to catch hell from peers.

INTERVIEWER

So every afternoon you would go to the *Echo* office—

VONNEGUT

Yeah. And one time, while I was writing, I happened to sniff my armpits absentmindedly. Several people saw me do it, and thought it was funny—and ever after that I was given the name "Snarf." In the annual for my graduating class, the class of 1940, I'm listed as "Kurt Snarfield Vonnegut, Jr." Technically, I wasn't really a snarf. A snarf was a person who went around sniffing girls' bicycle saddles. I didn't do that. "Twerp" also had a very specific meaning, which few people know now. Through careless usage, "twerp" is a pretty formless insult now.

INTERVIEWER

What is a twerp in the strictest sense, in the original sense?

VONNEGUT

It's a person who inserts a set of false teeth between the cheeks of his ass.

INTERVIEWER

I see.

VONNEGUT

I beg your pardon; between the cheeks of his or *her* ass. I'm always offending feminists that way.

INTERVIEWER

I don't quite understand why someone would do that with false teeth.

VONNEGUT

In order to bite the buttons off the backseats of taxicabs. That's the only reason twerps do it. It's all that turns them on.

INTERVIEWER

You went to Cornell University after Shortridge?

VONNEGUT

I imagine.

INTERVIEWER

You imagine?

VONNEGUT

I had a friend who was a heavy drinker. If somebody asked him if he'd been drunk the night before, he would always answer offhandedly, "Oh, I imagine." I've always liked that answer. It acknowledges life as a dream. Cornell was a boozy dream, partly because of booze itself, and partly because I was enrolled exclusively in courses I had no talent for. My father and brother agreed that I should study chemistry, since my brother had done so well with chemicals at M.I.T. He's eight years older than I am. Funnier, too. His most famous discovery is that silver iodide will sometimes make it rain or snow.

INTERVIEWER

Was your sister funny, too?

VONNEGUT

Oh, yes. There was an odd cruel streak to her sense of humor, though, which didn't fit in with the rest of her character somehow. She thought it was terribly funny whenever anybody fell down. One time she saw a woman come out of a streetcar horizontally, and she laughed for weeks after that.

INTERVIEWER

Horizontally?

VONNEGUT

Yes. This woman must have caught her heels somehow. Anyway, the streetcar door opened, and my sister happened to be watching from the sidewalk, and then she saw this woman come out horizontally—as straight as a board, face down, and about two feet off the ground.

INTERVIEWER

Slapstick?

VONNEGUT

Sure. We loved Laurel and Hardy. You know what one of the funniest things is that can happen in a film?

INTERVIEWER

No.

VONNEGUT

To have somebody walk through what looks like a shallow little puddle, but which is actually six feet deep. I remember a movie where Cary Grant was loping across lawns at night. He came to a low hedge, which he cleared ever so gracefully, only there was a twenty-foot drop on the other side. But the thing my sister and I loved best was when somebody in a movie would tell everybody off, and then make a grand exit into the coat closet. He had to come out again, of course, all tangled in coat hangers and scarves.

INTERVIEWER

Did you take a degree in chemistry at Cornell?

VONNEGUT

I was flunking everything by the middle of my junior year. I was delighted to join the army and go to war. After the war, I went to the University of Chicago, where I was pleased to study anthropology, a science that was mostly poetry, that involved almost no math at all. I was married by then, and soon had one kid, who was Mark. He would later go crazy, of course, and write a fine book about it—*The Eden Express*. He has just fathered a kid himself, my first grandchild, a boy named Zachary. Mark is finishing his second year in Harvard Medical School, and will be about the only member of his class not to be in debt when he graduates—because of the book. That's a pretty decent recovery from a crackup, I'd say.

INTERVIEWER

Did the study of anthropology later color your writings?

VONNEGUT

It confirmed my atheism, which was the faith of my fathers anyway. Religions were exhibited and studied as the Rube Goldberg inventions I'd always thought they were. We weren't allowed to find one culture superior to any other. We caught hell if we mentioned races much. It was highly idealistic.

INTERVIEWER

Almost a religion?

VONNEGUT

Exactly. And the only one for me. So far.

INTERVIEWER

What was your dissertation?

VONNEGUT

Cat's Cradle.

INTERVIEWER

But you wrote that years after you left Chicago, didn't you?

VONNEGUT

I left Chicago without writing a dissertation—and without a degree. All my ideas for dissertations had been rejected, and I was broke, so I took a job as a P.R. man for General Electric in Schenectady. Twenty years later, I got a letter from a new dean at Chicago, who had been looking through my dossier. Under the rules of the university, he said, a published work of high quality could be substituted for a dissertation, so I was entitled to an M.A. He had shown *Cat's Cradle* to the anthropology department, and they had said it was halfway decent anthropology, so they were mailing me my degree. I'm class of 1972 or so.

INTERVIEWER

Congratulations.

VONNEGUT

It was nothing, really. A piece of cake.

INTERVIEWER

Some of the characters in *Cat's Cradle* were based on people you knew at G.E., isn't that so?

VONNEGUT

Dr. Felix Hoenikker, the absentminded scientist, was a cari-
cature of Dr. Irving Langmuir, the star of the G.E. research
laboratory. I knew him some. My brother worked with him.
Langmuir was wonderfully absentminded. He wondered
out loud one time whether, when turtles pulled in their
heads, their spines buckled or contracted. I put that in the
book. One time he left a tip under his plate after his wife
served him breakfast at home. I put that in. His most important contribution, though, was the idea for what I called
"Ice-9," a form of frozen water that was stable at room temperature. He didn't tell it directly to me. It was a legend
around the laboratory—about the time H. G. Wells came
to Schenectady. That was long before my time. I was just a
little boy when it happened—listening to the radio, building model airplanes.

INTERVIEWER

Yes?

VONNEGUT

Anyway—Wells came to Schenectady, and Langmuir was
told to be his host. Langmuir thought he might entertain
Wells with an idea for a science-fiction story—about a form
of ice that was stable at room temperature. Wells was un-
interested, or at least never used the idea. And then Wells
died, and then, finally, Langmuir died. I thought to myself:
"Finders, keepers—the idea is mine." Langmuir, incidentally,

was the first scientist in private industry to win a Nobel Prize.

INTERVIEWER

How do you feel about Bellow's winning the Nobel Prize for Literature?

VONNEGUT

It was the best possible way to honor our entire literature.

INTERVIEWER

Do you find it easy to talk to him?

VONNEGUT

Yes. I've had about three opportunities. I was his host one time at the University of Iowa, where I was teaching and he was lecturing. It went very well. We had one thing in common, anyway—

INTERVIEWER

Which was—?

VONNEGUT

We were both products of the anthropology department of the University of Chicago. So far as I know, he never went on any anthropological expeditions, and neither did I. We invented preindustrial peoples instead—I in *Cat's Cradle* and he in *Henderson the Rain King*.

INTERVIEWER

So he is a fellow scientist.

VONNEGUT

I'm no scientist at all. I'm glad, though, now that I was pressured into becoming a scientist by my father and my brother. I understand how scientific reasoning and playfulness work, even though I have no talent for joining in. I enjoy the company of scientists, am easily excited and entertained when they tell me what they're doing. I've spent a lot more time with scientists than with literary people, my brother's friends, mostly. I enjoy plumbers and carpenters and automobile mechanics, too. I didn't get to know any literary people until the last ten years, starting with two years of teaching at Iowa. There at Iowa, I was suddenly friends with Nelson Algren and José Donoso and Vance Bourjaily and Donald Justice and George Starbuck and Marvin Bell, and so on. I was amazed. Now, judging from the reviews my latest book, *Slapstick,* has received, people would like to bounce me out of the literary establishment—send me back where I came from.

INTERVIEWER

There were some bad reviews?

VONNEGUT

Only in *The New York Times, Time, Newsweek, The New York Review of Books*, the *Village Voice*, and *Rolling Stone*. They loved me in Medicine Hat.

INTERVIEWER

To what do you attribute this rancor?

VONNEGUT

Slapstick may be a very bad book. I am perfectly willing
to believe that. Everybody else writes lousy books, so why
shouldn't I? What was unusual about the reviews was that
they wanted people to admit now that I had never been
any good. The reviewer for the Sunday *Times* actually asked
critics who had praised me in the past to now admit in public how wrong they'd been. My publisher, Sam Lawrence,
tried to comfort me by saying that authors were invariably
attacked when they became fabulously well-to-do.

INTERVIEWER

You needed comforting?

VONNEGUT

I never felt worse in my life. I felt as though I were sleeping
standing up on a boxcar in Germany again.

INTERVIEWER

That bad?

VONNEGUT

No. But bad enough. All of a sudden, critics wanted me
squashed like a bug. And it wasn't just that I had money all
of a sudden, either. The hidden complaint was that I was
barbarous, that I wrote without having made a systematic

study of great literature, that I was no gentleman, since I had done hack writing so cheerfully for vulgar magazines— that I had not paid my academic dues.

INTERVIEWER

You had not suffered?

VONNEGUT

I had suffered, all right—but as a badly educated person in vulgar company and in a vulgar trade. It was dishonorable enough that I perverted art for money. I then topped that felony by becoming, as I say, fabulously well-to-do. Well, that's just too damn bad for me and for everybody. I'm completely in print, so we're all stuck with me and stuck with my books.

INTERVIEWER

Do you mean to fight back?

VONNEGUT

In a way. I'm on the New York State Council for the Arts now, and every so often some other member talks about sending notices to college English departments about some literary opportunity, and I say, "Send them to the chemistry departments, send them to the zoology departments, send them to the anthropology departments and the astronomy departments and physics departments, and all the medical and law schools. That's where the writers are most likely to be."

INTERVIEWER

You believe that?

VONNEGUT

I think it can be tremendously refreshing if a creator of literature has something on his mind other than the history of literature so far. Literature should not disappear up its own asshole, so to speak.

INTERVIEWER

Let's talk about the women in your books.

VONNEGUT

There aren't any. No real women, no love.

INTERVIEWER

Is this worth expounding upon?

VONNEGUT

It's a mechanical problem. So much of what happens in storytelling is mechanical, has to do with the technical problems of how to make a story work. Cowboy stories and policeman stories end in shoot-outs, for example, because shoot-outs are the most reliable mechanisms for making such stories end. There is nothing like death to say what is always such an artificial thing to say: "The end." I try to keep deep love out of my stories because, once that particular subject comes up, it is almost impossible to talk about anything else. Readers don't want to hear about anything else. They go gaga about love. If a lover in a story wins his true love, that's the end of the tale, even if World War III is about to begin, and the sky is black with flying saucers.

INTERVIEWER

So you keep love out.

VONNEGUT

I have other things I want to talk about. Ralph Ellison did the same thing in *Invisible Man*. If the hero in that magnificent book had found somebody worth loving, somebody who was crazy about him, that would have been the end of the story. Céline did the same thing in *Journey to the End of Night:* he excluded the possibility of true and final love—so that the story could go on and on and on.

INTERVIEWER

Not many writers talk about the mechanics of stories.

VONNEGUT

I am such a barbarous technocrat that I believe they can be tinkered with like Model T Fords.

INTERVIEWER

To what end?

VONNEGUT

To give the reader pleasure.

INTERVIEWER

Will you ever write a love story, do you think?

VONNEGUT

Maybe. I lead a loving life. I really do. Even when I'm leading that loving life, though, and it's going so well, I sometimes find myself thinking, "My goodness, couldn't we
talk about something else for just a little while?" You know
what's really funny?

INTERVIEWER

No.

VONNEGUT

My books are being thrown out of school libraries all over
the country—because they're supposedly obscene. I've seen
letters to small-town newspapers that put *Slaughterhouse-
Five* in the same class with *Deep Throat* and *Hustler* magazine.
How could anybody masturbate to *Slaughterhouse-Five*?

INTERVIEWER

It takes all kinds.

VONNEGUT

Well, that kind doesn't exist. It's my religion the censors
hate. They find me disrespectful towards their idea of God
Almighty. They think it's the proper business of government
to protect the reputation of God. All I can say is, "Good
luck to them, and good luck to the government, and good

luck to God." You know what H. L. Mencken said one time about religious people? He said he'd been greatly misunderstood. He said he didn't hate them. He simply found them comical.

INTERVIEWER

When I asked you a while back which member of your family had influenced you most as a writer, you said your mother. I had expected you to say your sister, since you talked so much about her in *Slapstick*.

VONNEGUT

I said in *Slapstick* that she was the person I wrote for—that every successful creative person creates with an audience of one in mind. That's the secret of artistic unity. Anybody can achieve it, if he or she will make something with only one person in mind. I didn't realize that she was the person I wrote for until after she died.

INTERVIEWER

She loved literature?

VONNEGUT

She wrote wonderfully well. She didn't read much—but then again, neither in later years did Henry David Thoreau. My father was the same way: he didn't read much, but he could write like a dream. Such letters my father and sister wrote! When I compare their prose with mine, I am ashamed.

INTERVIEWER

Did your sister try to write for money, too?

VONNEGUT

No. She could have been a remarkable sculptor, too. I bawled her out one time for not doing more with the talents she had. She replied that having talent doesn't carry with it the obligation that something has to be done with it. This was startling news to me. I thought people were supposed to grab their talents and run as far and fast as they could.

INTERVIEWER

What do you think now?

VONNEGUT

Well—what my sister said now seems a peculiarly feminine sort of wisdom. I have two daughters who are as talented as she was, and both of them are damned if they are going to lose their poise and senses of humor by snatching up their talents and desperately running as far and as fast as they can. They saw me run as far and as fast as I could—and it must have looked like quite a crazy performance to them. And this is the worst possible metaphor, for what they actually saw was a man sitting still for decades.

INTERVIEWER

At a typewriter.

VONNEGUT

Yes, and smoking his fool head off.

INTERVIEWER

Have you ever stopped smoking?

VONNEGUT

Twice. Once I did it cold turkey, and turned into Santa Claus. I became roly-poly. I was approaching two hundred and fifty pounds. I stopped for almost a year, and then the University of Hawaii brought me to Oahu to speak. I was drinking out of a coconut on the roof of the Ili Kai one night, and all I had to do to complete the ring of my happiness was to smoke a cigarette. Which I did.

INTERVIEWER

The second time?

VONNEGUT

Very recently—last year. I paid Smokenders a hundred and fifty dollars to help me quit, over a period of six weeks. It was exactly as they had promised—easy and instructive. I won my graduation certificate and recognition pin. The only trouble was that I had also gone insane. I was supremely happy and proud, but those around me found me unbearably opinionated and abrupt and boisterous. Also: I had stopped writing. I didn't even write letters anymore. I had made a bad trade, evidently. So I started smoking again.

As the National Association of Manufacturers used to say, "There's no such thing as a free lunch."

INTERVIEWER
Do you really think creative writing can be taught?

VONNEGUT
About the same way golf can be taught. A pro can point out obvious flaws in your swing. I did that well, I think, at the University of Iowa for two years. Gail Godwin and John Irving and Jonathan Penner and Bruce Dobler and John Casey and Jane Casey were all students of mine out there. They've all published wonderful stuff since then. I taught creative writing badly at Harvard—because my marriage was breaking up, and because I was commuting every week to Cambridge from New York. I taught even worse at City College a couple of years ago. I had too many other projects going on at the same time. I don't have the will to teach anymore. I only know the theory.

INTERVIEWER
Could you put the theory into a few words?

VONNEGUT
It was stated by Paul Engle—the founder of the Writers Workshop at Iowa. He told me that, if the workshop ever got a building of its own, these words should be inscribed over the entrance: "Don't take it all so seriously."

INTERVIEWER

And how would that be helpful?

VONNEGUT

It would remind the students that they were learning to play practical jokes.

INTERVIEWER

Practical jokes?

VONNEGUT

If you make people laugh or cry about little black marks on sheets of white paper, what is that but a practical joke? All the great story lines are great practical jokes that people fall for over and over again.

INTERVIEWER

Can you give an example?

VONNEGUT

The Gothic novel. Dozens of the things are published every year, and they all sell. My friend Borden Deal recently wrote a Gothic novel for the fun of it, and I asked him what the plot was, and he said, "A young woman takes a job in an old house and gets the pants scared off her."

INTERVIEWER

Some more examples?

VONNEGUT

The others aren't that much fun to describe: somebody gets into trouble, and then gets out again; somebody loses something and gets it back; somebody is wronged and gets revenge; Cinderella; somebody hits the skids and just goes down, down, down; people fall in love with each other, and a lot of other people get in the way; a virtuous person is falsely accused of sin; a sinful person is believed to be virtuous; a person faces a challenge bravely, and succeeds or fails; a person lies, a person steals, a person kills, a person commits fornication.

INTERVIEWER

If you will pardon my saying so, these are very old-fashioned plots.

VONNEGUT

I guarantee you that no modern story scheme, even plotlessness, will give a reader genuine satisfaction, unless one of those old-fashioned plots is smuggled in somewhere. I don't praise plots as accurate representations of life, but as ways to keep readers reading. When I used to teach creative writing, I would tell the students to make their characters want something right away—even if it's only a glass of water. Characters paralyzed by the meaninglessness of modern life still have to drink water from time to time. One of my students wrote a story about a nun who got a piece of dental floss stuck between her lower left molars, and who couldn't get it out all day long. I thought that was wonderful. The story dealt with issues a lot more important than dental floss, but what kept readers going was anxiety about when the dental floss would finally be removed. Nobody could read that story without fishing around in his mouth with a finger. Now, there's an admirable practical joke for you. When you exclude plot, when you exclude anyone's wanting anything, you exclude the reader, which is a mean-spirited thing to do. You can also exclude the reader by not telling him immediately where the story is taking place, and who the people are—

INTERVIEWER

And what they want.

VONNEGUT

Yes. And you can put him to sleep by never having characters confront each other. Students like to say that they stage no confrontations because people avoid confrontations in modern life. "Modern life is so lonely," they say. This is laziness. It's the writer's job to stage confrontations, so the characters will say surprising and revealing things, and educate and entertain us all. If a writer can't or won't do that, he should withdraw from the trade.

INTERVIEWER

Trade?

VONNEGUT

Trade. Carpenters build houses. Storytellers use a reader's

leisure time in such a way that the reader will not feel that his time has been wasted. Mechanics fix automobiles.

INTERVIEWER

Surely talent is required?

VONNEGUT

In all those fields. I was a Saab dealer on Cape Cod for a while, and I enrolled in their mechanic's school, and they threw me out of their mechanic's school. No talent.

INTERVIEWER

How common is storytelling talent?

VONNEGUT

In a creative writing class of twenty people anywhere in this country, six students will be startlingly talented. Two of those might actually publish something by and by.

INTERVIEWER

What distinguishes those two from the rest?

VONNEGUT

They will have something other than literature itself on their minds. They will probably be hustlers, too. I mean that they won't want to wait passively for somebody to discover them. They will insist on being read.

INTERVIEWER

You have been a public relations man and an advertising man—

VONNEGUT

Oh, I imagine.

INTERVIEWER

Was this painful? I mean—did you feel your talent was being wasted, being crippled?

VONNEGUT

No. That's romance—that work of that sort damages a writer's soul. At Iowa, Dick Yates and I used to give a lecture each year on the writer and the free-enterprise system. The students hated it. We would talk about all the hack jobs writers could take in case they found themselves starving to death, or in case they wanted to accumulate enough capital to finance the writing of a book. Since publishers aren't putting money into first novels anymore, and since the magazines have died, and since television isn't buying from young freelancers anymore, and since the foundations give grants only to old poops like me, young writers are going to have to support themselves as shameless hacks. Otherwise, we are soon going to find ourselves without a contemporary literature. There is only one genuinely ghastly thing hack jobs do to writers, and that is to waste their precious time.

INTERVIEWER

No joke.

VONNEGUT

A tragedy. I just keep trying to think of ways, even horrible ways, for young writers to somehow hang on.

INTERVIEWER

Should young writers be subsidized?

VONNEGUT

Something's got to be done, now that free enterprise has made it impossible for them to support themselves through free enterprise. I was a sensational businessman in the beginning—for the simple reason that there was so much business to be done. When I was working for General Electric, I wrote a story, "Report on the Barnhouse Effect," the first story I ever wrote. I mailed it off to *Collier's*. Knox Burger was fiction editor there. Knox told me what was wrong with it and how to fix it. I did what he said, and he bought the story for seven hundred and fifty dollars, six weeks' pay at G.E. I wrote another, and he paid me nine hundred and fifty dollars, and suggested that it was perhaps time for me to quit G.E. Which I did. I moved to Provincetown. Eventually, my price for a short story got up to twenty-nine hundred dollars a crack. Think of that. And Knox got me a couple of agents who were as shrewd about storytelling as he was—Kenneth Littauer, who had been his predecessor at *Collier's,* and Max Wilkinson, who had been a story editor for MGM. And let it be put on the record here that Knox Burger, who is about my age, discovered and encouraged more good young writers than any other editor of his time. I don't think that's ever been written down anywhere. It's a fact known only to writers, and one that could easily vanish, if it isn't somewhere written down.

INTERVIEWER

Where is Knox Burger now?

VONNEGUT

He's a literary agent. He represents my son Mark, in fact.

INTERVIEWER

And Littauer and Wilkinson?

VONNEGUT

Littauer died ten years ago or so. He was a colonel in the Lafayette Escadrille, by the way, at the age of twenty-three—and the first man to strafe a trench. He was my mentor. Max Wilkinson has retired to Florida. It always embarrassed him to be an agent. If some stranger asked him what he did for a living, he always said he was a cotton planter.

INTERVIEWER

Do you have a new mentor now?

VONNEGUT

No. I guess I'm too old to find one. Whatever I write now

is set in type without comment by my publisher, who is younger than I am, by editors, by anyone. I don't have my sister to write for anymore. Suddenly, there are all these unfilled jobs in my life.

INTERVIEWER

Do you feel as though you're up there without a net under you?

VONNEGUT

And without a balancing pole, either. It gives me the heebie-jeebies sometimes.

INTERVIEWER

Is there anything else you'd like to add?

VONNEGUT

You know the panic bars they have on the main doors of schools and theaters? If you get slammed into the door, the door will fly open?

INTERVIEWER

Yes.

VONNEGUT

The brand name on most of them is "Von Duprin." The "Von" is for Vonnegut. A relative of mine was caught in the Iroquois Theater Fire in Chicago a long time ago, and he

invented the panic bar along with two other guys. "Prin"
was Prinzler. I forget who "Du" was.

INTERVIEWER
Okay.

VONNEGUT
And I want to say, too, that humorists are very commonly
the youngest children in their families. When I was the lit-
tlest kid at our supper table, there was only one way I could
get anybody's attention, and that was to be funny. I had to
specialize. I used to listen to radio comedians very intently,
so I could learn how to make jokes. And that's what my
books are, now that I'm a grownup—mosaics of jokes.

INTERVIEWER
Do you have any favorite jokes?

VONNEGUT
My sister and I used to argue about what the funniest joke
in the world was—next to a guy storming into a coat closet,
of course. When the two of us worked together, incidentally, we could be almost as funny as Laurel and Hardy.
That's basically what *Slapstick* was about.

INTERVIEWER
Did you finally agree on the world's champion joke?

VONNEGUT

We finally settled on two. It's sort of hard to tell either one just flat-footed like this.

INTERVIEWER

Do it anyway.

VONNEGUT

Well—you won't laugh. Nobody ever laughs. But one is an old "Two Black Crows" joke. The "Two Black Crows" were white guys in blackface—named Moran and Mack. They made phonograph records of their routines, two supposedly black guys talking lazily to each other. Anyway, one of them says, "Last night I dreamed I was eating flannel cakes." The other one says, "Is that so?" And the first one says, "And when I woke up, the blanket was gone."

INTERVIEWER

Um.

VONNEGUT

I told you you wouldn't laugh. The other champion joke requires your cooperation. I will ask you a question, and you will have to say "No."

INTERVIEWER

Okay.

VONNEGUT

Do you know why cream is so much more expensive than milk?

INTERVIEWER

No.

VONNEGUT

Because the cows hate to squat on those little bottles. See, you didn't laugh again, but I give you my sacred word of honor that those are splendid jokes. Exquisite craftsmanship.

INTERVIEWER

You seem to prefer Laurel and Hardy over Chaplin. Is that so?

VONNEGUT

I'm crazy about Chaplin, but there's too much distance between him and his audience. He is too obviously a genius. In his own way, he's as brilliant as Picasso, and this is intimidating to me.

INTERVIEWER

Will you ever write another short story?

VONNEGUT

Maybe. I wrote what I thought would be my last one about eight years ago. Harlan Ellison asked me to contribute to a collection he was making. The story's called "The Big Space Fuck." I think I am the first writer to use "fuck" in a title. It

was about firing a spaceship with a warhead full of jizzum at
Andromeda. Which reminds me of my good Indianapolis
friend, about the only Indianapolis friend I've got left—
William Failey. When we got into the Second World War,
and everybody was supposed to give blood, he wondered if
he couldn't give a pint of jizzum instead.

INTERVIEWER

If your parents hadn't lost all their money, what would you
be doing now?

VONNEGUT

I'd be an Indianapolis architect—like my father and grandfather. And very happy, too. I still wish that had happened.
One thing, anyway: One of the best young architects out
there lives in a house my father built for our family the year
I was born—1922. My initials, and my sister's initials, and
my brother's initials are all written in leaded glass in the
three little windows by the front door.

INTERVIEWER

So you have good old days you hanker for.

VONNEGUT

Yes. Whenever I go to Indianapolis, the same question
asks itself over and over again in my head: "Where's my
bed, where's my bed?" And if my father's and grandfather's
ghosts haunt that town, they must be wondering where all
their buildings have gone to. The center of the city, where

most of their buildings were, has been turned into park-
ing lots. They must be wondering where all their relatives
went, too. They grew up in a huge extended family which
is no more. I got the slightest taste of that—the big family
thing. And when I went to the University of Chicago, and I
heard the head of the Department of Anthropology, Robert
Redfield, lecture on the folk society, which was essentially a
stable, isolated extended family, he did not have to tell me
how nice that could be.

INTERVIEWER

Anything else?

VONNEGUT

Well—I just discovered a prayer for writers. I'd heard of
prayers for sailors and kings and soldiers and so on—but
never of a prayer for writers. Could I put that in here?

INTERVIEWER

Certainly.

VONNEGUT

It was written by Samuel Johnson on April 3, 1753, the day
on which he signed a contract which required him to write
the first complete dictionary of the English language. He
was praying for himself. Perhaps April third should be cel-
ebrated as "Writers' Day." Anyway, this is the prayer: "O
God, who hast hitherto supported me, enable me to pro-
ceed in this labor, and in the whole task of my present state;

that when I shall render up, at the last day, an account of the talent committed to me, I may receive pardon, for the sake of Jesus Christ. Amen."

INTERVIEWER

That seems to be a wish to carry his talent as far and as fast as he can.

VONNEGUT

Yes. He was a notorious hack.

INTERVIEWER

And you consider yourself a hack?

VONNEGUT

Of a sort.

INTERVIEWER

What sort?

VONNEGUT

A child of the Great Depression. And perhaps we should say something at this point how this interview itself was done—unless candor would somehow spoil everything.

INTERVIEWER

Let the chips fall where they may.

VONNEGUT

Four different interviews with me were submitted to *The*

Paris Review. These were patched together to form a single interview, which was shown to me. This scheme worked only fairly well, so I called in yet another interviewer to make it all of a piece. I was that person. With utmost tenderness, I interviewed myself.

INTERVIEWER

I see. Our last question. If you were Commissar of Publishing in the United States, what would you do to alleviate the present deplorable situation?

VONNEGUT

There is no shortage of wonderful writers. What we lack is a dependable mass of readers.

INTERVIEWER

So—?

VONNEGUT

I propose that every person out of work be required to submit a book report before he or she gets his or her welfare check.

INTERVIEWER

Thank you.

VONNEGUT

Thank *you*.

"THERE MUST BE MORE TO LOVE THAN DEATH"

INTERVIEW BY ROBERT K. MUSIL

FIRST PUBLISHED IN *THE NATION*
AUGUST 2-9, 1980 ISSUE

MUSIL: It must have been difficult to work up to a book like *Slaughterhouse-Five*. How long did you think about describing an experience like Dresden?

VONNEGUT: Well, it seemed a categorical imperative that I write about Dresden, the firebombing of Dresden, since it was the largest massacre in the history of Europe and I am a person of European extraction and I, a writer, had been present. I *had* to say something about it. And it took me a long time and it was painful. The most difficult thing about it was that I had forgotten about it. And I learned about catastrophes from that, and from talking to other people who had been involved in avalanches and floods and great fires, that there is some device in our brain which switches off and prevents our remembering catastrophes above a certain scale. I don't know whether it is just a limitation of our nervous system, or whether it's actually a gadget which protects us in some way. But I, in fact, remembered nothing about the bombing of Dresden although I had been there, and did everything short of hiring a hypnotist to recover the information. I wrote to many of the guys who went through it with me saying "Help me remember" and the answer every time was a refusal, a simple flat refusal. They did not want to think about it. There was a writer in *Life* magazine—I don't know how much he knows about rabbits and the nervous system—who claimed that rabbits have no memory, which is one of their defensive mechanisms. If they recalled every close shave they had in the course of just an hour, life would become insupportable. As soon as they'd escaped from a Doberman Pinscher, why, they forgot all about it. And they could scarcely afford to remember it.

MUSIL: Did the details come back to you personally when you wrote to people and studied about Dresden? You said it was painful when you started thinking about it again.

VONNEGUT: After all, it was a city enormous in area and I was on the ground, and there was smoke and fire, and so I could scarcely see eight feet, and the only way to see it would be on area photographs taken with the beautiful equipment that planes had. And so it was finally British military historians who produced more and more information and finally an estimate of the casualties. East Germany would not respond to my inquiries at all. They weren't interested in the problem. Probably the most curious thing, in retrospect, is that I think that I'm the only person who gives a damn that Dresden was bombed, because I have found no Germans to mourn the city, no Englishmen. I have run into flyers of one sort or another who were in on the raid. They were rather sheepish about it, and they weren't proud of it. But I have found no one who is sorry, including the people who were bombed, although they must surely mourn relatives. I went back there with a friend and there was no German to say, "Ach, how beautiful this used to be, with the tree-lined streets and the parks." They don't give a damn. And there was a special edition of *Slaughterhouse-Five* that the Franklin Library brought out. For that, I had to write a special introduction for their subscribers, and I figured out that I'm the only person who profited from the bombing of Dresden. I estimated at the time I got about $4 for each person killed.

MUSIL: In the course of doing this series, I've interviewed people who have observed massive bombing. You weren't a bomber, but you had direct experience with bombing. I wonder if your experience in Dresden led you to any special interest (that's a bloodless way of saying it) in Hiroshima, or in subjects like nuclear weapons. Is there some connection in your mind, as in *Cat's Cradle*?

VONNEGUT: Well, the interest would have been there in any event, I think. Dresden wasn't all that instructive. It was a coincidence in my life. But I think I would have been a pacifist anyway. I'm technologically educated—I'm educated as a chemist, not as a writer. I was studying chemistry at the time and was from a technocratic family. During the Depression we really believed that scientists and engineers should be put in charge and that a technological utopia was possible. My brother, who is nine years older than I am, became a distinguished scientist. He's Dr. Bernard Vonnegut, who got a Ph.D. from the Massachusetts Institute of Technology. The flashiest thing he discovered was that silver iodide will make it snow and rain. That's his patent. He is actually a leading atmospheric chemist now.

But for me it was terrible, after having believed so much in technology and having drawn so many pictures of dream automobiles and dream airplanes and dream human dwellings, to see the actual use of this technology in destroying a city and killing 135,000 people and then to see the even more sophisticated technology in the use of nuclear weapons on Japan. I was sickened by this use of the technology that I had had such great hopes for. And so I came to fear it. You know, it's like being a devout Christian and then seeing some horrible massacres conducted by Christians after a victory. It was a spiritual horror of that sort which I still carry today...

MUSIL: You mentioned religious and philosophical values. At the end of *Cat's Cradle*, Bokonon talking about writing the history of human stupidity...

VONNEGUT: There actually is a book called that, you know. It's called the *Short Introduction to the History of Human Stupidity*, by Walter Pitkin, and it was published during the '30s. The most horrible hypocrisy or the most terrifying hypocrisy or the most tragic hypocrisy at the center of life, I think, which no one dares mention, is that human beings don't like life. Bertrand Russell skirted that, and many psychoanalysts have too, in talking about people lusting for death. But I think that at least half the people alive, and maybe nine-tenths of them, really do not like this ordeal at all. They pretend to like it some, to smile at strangers, and to get up each morning in order to survive, in order to somehow get through it. But life is, for most people, a very terrible ordeal. They would just as soon end it at any time. And I think that is more of a problem really than greed or machismo or anything like that. You know, you talk about the dark side of life: that's really it. Most people don't want to be alive. They're too embarrassed, they're disgraced, they're frightened. I think that's the fundamental thing that's going on. Those of you with your devotion to peace and all that are actually facing people perhaps as brave and determined and resourceful and thoughtful as you are on some level. And what they really want to do is to have the whole thing turned off like a light switch.

MUSIL: So would you consider yourself a fatalist? Throughout your books, there is the phrase, "So it goes." But what is that theme, that leitmotif? What does it indicate about your own thinking about where we're headed, armed with our nuclear weapons?

VONNEGUT: When I'm engaged in any action I have to take into consideration that many of the people on either side of me don't care what happens next. I am mistrustful of most people as custodians of life and so I'm pessimistic on that account. I think that there are not many people who want life to go on. And I'm just a bearer of bad tidings really. You know, I just got born myself and this is what I found on this particular planet. But life is very unpopular here, and maybe it will be different on the next one.

MUSIL: *Cat's Cradle* features a narrator who is ostensibly working on a book about the day the bomb went off at Hiroshima, and trying to find out what the people did, including great scientists like Dr. Felix Hoenikker, your fictional father of the bomb. What is the germ of that novel, and why did you pick that kind of focus?

VONNEGUT: I was a public relations man for the General Electric Company's research laboratory, which happens to be an extremely interesting research laboratory. As General Electric found out, it was very profitable to hire scientists from M.I.T. or Princeton or wherever and say, "Hey, you don't have to teach anymore; you can do research all day long, and we won't tell you what to do. We will simply buy you the equipment." The job required my visiting the scientists often and talking to them and asking them what they were up to. Every so often a good story would come out of it. I got to know these people, and the older ones began to trouble me a lot; not the younger ones, but the older ones began to believe the truth must be served and that they need not fear whatever they turned up in the course of their research. And a man that my brother worked with there, a Nobel Prize winner named Irving Langmuir, was more or less the model for Felix Hoenikker. Langmuir was absolutely indifferent to the uses that might be made of the truths he dug out of the rock and handed out to whomever was around. But any truth he found was beautiful in its own right, and he didn't give a damn who got it next.

I think we live more according to literary stereotypes and dramatic stereotypes than we know. I think there were literary models then of pure scientists and their absent-mindedness, and jokes about the absent-minded professor and all that, and many scientists gladly fell into this stereotype of absent-mindedness and indifference, including indifference as to what became of their discoveries. That generation was not cautious at all about what information it turned over to the Government, to the War Department, to the Secretary of the Army or whomever. But one member of that generation, Norbert Weiner, published an article in *The Atlantic* not long after the war was over, saying, "I'm not going to tell my Government anything anymore." And I think scientists have become more and more cautious since. I know my brother has. He was deeply chagrined to find out that the Air Force had been spewing silver iodide all over Vietnam in an effort to bring those people to their knees. You know this is preposterous. He says they might as well have been spewing paprika or something like that, hoping this would have some horrible effect on the enemy. But it sickened him to hear that they had hoped that his invention would have some destructive use.

MUSIL: If one of the problems as you saw it after the war was technocrats gone wild, what alternative do you propose in your literature or in your own thinking? What did you decide was the opposite or the antidote to the Felix Hoenikkers of the world?

VONNEGUT: Well, I encourage restraint. I think the trouble with Dresden was restraint surely, or lack of restraint, and don't regard technocrats as having gone mad. I think the politicians went mad, as they often do. The man responsible for the bombing of Dresden against a lot of advice was Winston Churchill. It's the brain of one man, the rage of one man, the pride of one man, and I really can't hold scientists particularly responsible for that.

MUSIL: But you do say, or at least the narrator says in *Cat's Cradle*, that Hoenikker couldn't have been all that innocent if he was the father of the A-bomb.

VONNEGUT: Well, what I feel about him now is that he was allowed to concentrate on one part of life more than any human being should be allowed to do. He was overspecialized and became amoral on that account. It would seem perfectly all right to see a musician vanish into his own world entirely. But if a scientist does this, he can inadvertently become a very destructive person.

MUSIL: How do you view a subject like the threat of nuclear war? Do you think the threat is increasing and do you worry about that?

VONNEGUT: Well, yes, indeed I do. I worry again about the indifference of people to it. You can talk about the various readings of *Dr. Strangelove* in that movie, and I tell you that the thing that satisfied the audience most was the beautiful end of the world, and playing that sentimental song over it. It was meant to be irony, but to most people in the audience and on most people's level it was beautiful. And I don't mean simple-minded people. I mean that this was stirring and lovely and appealing—the end of the world—and did not cause anyone to recoil from it. Now, there has been one bombing picture which does make you recoil from war, which is *The War Game*. That was extraordinary, and that was intolerable to people because it revealed how slow the death was going to be, the slow death of children and that sort of thing. That was bad news to people, but the peaceful end, the painless end was deeply gratifying to people, more so than all the Peter Sellers acting triumphs, more than the great Keenan Wynn jokes or shooting the coin box off the Coca-Cola machine. I'm afraid that beautiful ending is the reason that picture is so loved. Inadvertently, or maybe on purpose, Kubrick made a picture which sent people home utterly satisfied. And I'm sure that everyone that ever sees that picture sleeps soundly afterward and feels nothing more needs to be done.

MUSIL: How about your books, particularly *Slaughterhouse-Five*? How do you think people react to the sort of destruction depicted there?

VONNEGUT: I have really no way of knowing. I haven't talked to that many readers, but I do hear from young people who say, "My father says the war wasn't that way at all." And the German response to it has been, "No, no, the war wasn't like that." Of course, damn it, I did as good research as they did about what the war was like and what the bombing of Dresden was like. But the Germans feel, you know, it's more or less their copyrighted war, and how dare I comment on it.

MUSIL: Apart from your role as a writer, do you concern yourself in other ways with the matter of nuclear weapons and their proliferation?

VONNEGUT: Well, for one thing, I've reproduced. I have children and I'm very fond of them and I want them to like life. I don't want them to lose heart. As for nuclear weapons, I can't imagine why anyone wants them. I don't want my country to have them. I don't want anybody to have them. And there's no point in going country by country by country because if they exist anywhere, they threaten the entire planet. So I don't want my planet to have them, and I think the people who don't feel they are particularly dangerous must be imbeciles or hypocrites. Or again, perhaps they're sick enough to want an end to life.

MUSIL: But what about a lively man like John F. Kennedy? Have you thought about his behavior during the Cuban missile crisis and ever wondered what was going on with someone who could sit and say, Well, we might just have to do it?

VONNEGUT: Well, this is the hypocrisy I'm talking about. When I see people with a lust for life climbing mountains or going hand over hand and doing these great acts of derring-do, showing their teeth, you know, and gnashing their teeth and loving steaks and loving women and loving whiskey and loving all of this, I become somewhat alarmed because I think perhaps that is a symptom of the hypocrisy—a person who pretends to like life and in fact overdoes it as though he or she had something to hide.

MUSIL: Since you have spent many years trying to understand both an event like the bombing of Dresden and the nature of scientists who could make Ice Nine or father atomic bombs, what do you think about when you hear the language of policy makers, people who talk about the bomb or nuclear weapons as a deterrent and so on?

VONNEGUT: Only about their willingness to lie, it being a normal part of politics to lie. I have a friend I went through the war with. We were scouts together, and then we were prisoners of war together. He's since become a district attorney in Pennsylvania; he's a guy named Bernie O'Hare. We came home on a troopship together and got off at Newport News. I said, "All right, what did you learn from it?" meaning World War II. We were both privates. He thought a minute and said, "I'll never believe my Government again."

During the '30s when we grew up, we did believe our Government and were great enthusiasts for it because the economy was being reborn. We were such cooperative citizens that it turned out to be a rather minor thing that made us decide that we couldn't believe our Government anymore—that we had caught it lying. It was quite something to catch your Government lying then. What it was all about was our bombing techniques. They said we had these magnificent bombsights which would allow us to drop a bomb down a smoke stack, and that there was all this microsurgery going on on the ground. Then we saw what it really was. They would send a cloud of airplanes over and bomb the shit out of everything. There was no use of bombsights whatsoever, there was simply carpet bombing. And that was kept secret from the American people: the nature of the air raids and random bombings, the shooting and the blowing up of anything that moved.

MUSIL: Did you accept the official Truman-Stimson explanation of the bombing of Hiroshima at first, or was that a fairly transparent lie to you?

VONNEGUT: I had already gotten off the troopship. I was liberated in May and didn't get home until the middle of June. But the bomb was dropped in August, and I was home on leave then. I had seen bombings, so when Truman spoke of marshaling yards and all these other military targets that had to be hit there in Hiroshima, I knew what bullshit it was, because anything is a marshaling yard, any building that stands is an offense, any wire that still hangs between two poles is an offense. But there are all these names that can be given to them. What sticks in my mind is that Truman had talked about the targets we had been after at Hiroshima, and spoke of the marshaling yards. You know there are marshaling yards in New York and there are marshaling yards in Indianapolis and there are marshaling yards in South Bend. I think they're just railroad yards, but there's this terrible thing if you marshal in them.

MUSIL: To move to the present, when you heard Jimmy Carter say in his inaugural address, "We hope to move toward our ultimate goal of zero nuclear weapons," did you automatically dismiss the statement? Do you think the public has begun to expect dishonest language from Government leaders?

VONNEGUT: Well, it's *thoughts* which are not taken seriously now. Orwell dealt in detail with language and the misuse of words. But he's talking about euphemisms, which is just disguising an unpleasant truth. As a matter of fact, if you go over a euphemistic sentence and put it into street English, well, then you can learn from it. You can simply decode it and get an offensive truth out of it. But I'm just talking about lies. There's no need for euphemisms anymore. The day of euphemisms is over. Now we hear total untruths. So there's no way to really crack the code except to suspect that the intent was to deceive.

MUSIL: Let me turn to a final question. Is there a way to let people know about the nuclear threat, really know that the world may blow up, without turning them off psychologically? Suppose I came to you for advice and said, "Look, I would like to alert people that there are these nuclear weapons out there and I might do a movie or write some poetry or go give speeches—how can it best be done?"

VONNEGUT: You are, and people like you are, crying in the wilderness and everything else is a rock or a tree, I think. And again, as I say, there are very few enthusiasts for life. It's as though you were just crazy about mah-jongg. If everybody would play mah-jongg, this might bring back the mah-jongg rage of the '20s. And, Jesus, nobody else will look at the tiles or pay attention; they don't care. They're not into that particular sport, and your particular sport is survival. It's one more game, and most people don't care to play it.

MUSIL: What does that lead *you* to conclude? Since your experience in World War II, we've gone from blockbusters then single, so-called puny atomic bombs of only twelve kilotons, to megatons, and now there are some 50,000 of them in the world. Do you ever think personally, "We're not going to make it"?

VONNEGUT: Well, we have made it. I mean, here we are. We're still alive, aren't we? We have survived, and how long we're supposed to do this, I don't know. It seems to me the whole world is living like Alcoholics Anonymous now, which is one day at a time, and it seems to me that President Carter is living that way too. Every night when he goes to bed he cackles, "By God, we made it through another day! Everybody said I was a lousy President, and here we've survived another day. That's not bad." We are living day by day by day now, but there seems to be very little restraint in the world. What an alcoholic does every day is not take a drink, and only not take a drink for a day. But I see no such real restraint with regard to warlike actions. If we were truly interested in surviving, and having sobriety, each day we would congratulate ourselves not for merely having gotten through another day but for making it without a warlike gesture. But there is no such restraint. More weapons are manufactured every day and more arguments are gladly entered into and more enormous, dangerous lies are told, so there is no restraint. It would be truly wonderful if we could live as alcoholics do, to be unwarlike for just another day. We don't. We're totally warlike, and sooner or later something's going to go wrong. The book I'm working on now is about a kid, he's grown now, grown and in his 40s and his father was a gun nut. It was a house with dozens of guns in it. At the age of 11 this kid was playing with one of his father's guns, which he wasn't supposed to do, put a cartridge into a 30-06 rifle and fired out a goddamn attic window and killed a housewife, you know, eighteen blocks away, just drilled her right between the eyes. And this has colored his whole life, and made his reputation. And of course this weapon should not have existed. He was brought into planet where this terribly unstable device existed, and all he had to do was sneeze near it. I mean, it wanted to be fired; it was built to be fired. It had no other purpose than to be fired and the existence of such an unstable device within the reach of any sort of human being is intolerable.

THE JOE & KURT SHOW

A CONVERSATION WITH KURT
VONNEGUT AND JOSEPH HELLER
WITH CAROLE MALLORY

FIRST PUBLISHED IN *PLAYBOY* 39:5
MAY 1992

We are settled on the patio of Joe's house in Amagansett on Long Island. Kurt sits in the shade, Joe nearer the lawn and in the sun. Both men wear khaki shorts.

PLAYBOY: You said last night that Joe was older.

HELLER: It depends on how we feel at the time.

VONNEGUT: Based on the thickness of his books, he's senior.

HELLER: You probably worked it out to the number of pages. You have twenty-seven books. They're all short. I have five books. They're all long.

PLAYBOY: How long have you been friends?

HELLER: I don't think we're friends now. I see him maybe twice a year.

VONNEGUT: We're associates. We're colleagues.

HELLER: We call each other when one of us needs something.

VONNEGUT: I don't know. We were both sort of PR people and promotional people at one time. I used to work for GE and I had ambitions to be a writer and I'd go to New York. I'd say we probably met about 1955 or so.

HELLER: No, no, I didn't meet you then. I met you at Notre Dame.

VONNEGUT: When was that?

HELLER: It was 1968, when Martin Luther King was shot. He was shot the night we were there. I remember flying back from South Bend to Chicago with Ralph Ellison and reading the papers. They were worrying that Chicago was on fire. I think he was supposed to stop there and decided not to. So that would be the time I met you. And that turned out to be a cataclysmic year. Bobby Kennedy was shot in 1968. Martin Luther King. The Soviets invaded Czechoslovakia.

VONNEGUT: Can I tell the story about you and the shooting of Martin Luther King?

HELLER: No. Of course you can.

VONNEGUT: It was a literary festival at Notre Dame and it went on for about three or four days and we took turns going on stage. It was Heller's turn to be screamingly funny and he got up there and he was just about to speak, no doubt with prepared material, and some sort of academic, a professor, came up over the footlights to the lectern and shouldered Joe aside politely and said, "I just want to announce that Martin Luther King has been shot." And then this guy went back over the footlights and took his seat, and Heller said, "Oh, my God. Oh, my God. I wish I were with Shirley now. She's crying her eyes out."

HELLER: Shirley was my first wife. And then I went into my prepared speech. It was a tough beginning. That's how we met. Kurt Vonnegut gave a speech that was probably the best speech I've ever heard. I think I haven't heard a better one since. He was so casual and so funny and it all seemed extemporaneous and when I came up afterward to shake his hand, I noticed he was drenched with sweat. I asked him a few years later if he had written the speech or was speaking off the cuff.

VONNEGUT: Every writer has to write his speech.

HELLER: I don't do that.

VONNEGUT: You don't?

HELLER: Nope. I have only one speech I give depending on whether or not Martin Luther King has been shot that day.

PLAYBOY: Would you like to give a speech now?

HELLER: Nope. I get paid for the speeches. And it's still nothing compared to what Ollie North gets when he's in his prime. Or Leona Helmsley—she can get more than that. Usually there is a year when certain people are very hot. Angela Davis was. Abbie Hoffman was.

VONNEGUT: Bork had about six months. But that was a scandal.

HELLER: I don't think it's a scandal.

VONNEGUT: The students come only to see reputed pinwheels and freaks. If you get an enormously dignified, intelligent, experienced man like Harrison Salisbury, nobody comes.

HELLER: You have a small audience and a few people walking out.

VONNEGUT: The best audience in the world is the 92nd Street Y. Those people know everything and they are wide awake and responsive.

HELLER: I was part of a panel there on December seventh. The fiftieth anniversary of Pearl Harbor.

VONNEGUT: Were you bombed at Pearl Harbor, Joe?

HELLER: No.

VONNEGUT: Of course, James Jones was. I was saying this would be sort of a valedictory interview because our generation is taking its leave now. James Jones is gone. Irwin Shaw is gone. Truman Capote is gone.

HELLER: Yeah, but nobody's replaced us.

VONNEGUT: No. (Laughter)

HELLER: By the way, that's the subject of a novel I'm doing now to be called *Closing Time*. It has to do with a person about my age realizing not only that he's way past his prime but also that life is nearing its end. The aptness of the invitation from the Y fits in because this novel begins with these lines, "When people my age speak of the war, it's not of Vietnam, but the one that broke out a half a century ago."

PLAYBOY: What are you working on, Kurt?

VONNEGUT: On a divorce. Which is a full-time job. Didn't you find it a full-time job?

HELLER: Oh, it's more than a full-time job. You ought to go back and read that section in *No Laughing Matter* on the divorce. I went through all the lawyers. But yours is going to be a tranquil one, you told me.

VONNEGUT: It seems to me divorce is so common now. It

ought to be more institutionalized. It's like a head-on colli-
sion every time. It's supposed to be a surprise but it's com-
monplace. Deliver your line about never having dreamed
of being married.

HELLER: It's in *Something Happened*: "I want a divorce; I
dream of a divorce. I was never sure I wanted to get married.
But I always knew I wanted a divorce."

VONNEGUT: Norman Mailer has what—five divorces now?

HELLER: One of my idols used to be Artie Shaw. He used to
marry these beautiful women who were very famous and be
able to afford to divorce them. At that time, divorces were
hard to get. You had to go to Nevada. The second thing,
you needed a great deal of alimony because the women
were always getting it. And I was wondering how a clarinet player could afford—was it Ava Gardner? Lana Turner?
Kathleen Winsor? Oh, I've forgotten the others. He had
about eight wives. All glamorous.

VONNEGUT: I used to play the clarinet and I thought he was
the greatest clarinet player ever.

HELLER: You thought he was a better clarinetist than Benny
Goodman or Pee Wee Russell?

VONNEGUT: It was explained to me by some musicologist. I
said to him, "I've got these vaudeville turns and the clarinet

thing is one of them," and he said, "Shaw used a special reed that nobody else used and a special mouthpiece that allowed him to get a full octave above what other people were playing." And that's what I kept hearing him do. Christ, he was getting way up there where nobody else was getting. But no, I think probably the greatest clarinet player in history was Benny Goodman.

HELLER: I would think so.

VONNEGUT: I wound up going home from Mailer's one time in a limo with Goodman and I said to him, "I used to play a little licorice stick myself."

PLAYBOY: Why are men more readily able than women to distinguish the difference between sex and love?

HELLER: Your question implies that when a woman engages in sex, she does so only when she's in love. Or she thinks of it as an act of love. Our vocabulary has become corrupt in a way that's embarrassing to me. Have you ever heard a man use the word "lover" about a woman? Have you ever heard a man say, "This gal, she's my lover?"

VONNEGUT: I'll say it of a woman. To close friends.

HELLER: I used the word only once in a book, when the character Gold is reacting exactly the way I am and the woman says, "You are my lover." He never thought of

himself as a lover. He says he always thought of himself as
a fucker, not a lover.

VONNEGUT: Well, this is Joe. Joe doesn't vote either. Is that
right, Joe?

HELLER: I will say—*Sound of a lawn mower*—Oh, shit! Is
he coming to do the lawn now? He is.

PLAYBOY: Shall we stop him? Or shall we go inside?

HELLER: We can go over there. No, we can't stop him.
You're lucky to get him.

*We move inside Heller's modern country home. Kurt sits on a
hassock between two sofas. Joe reclines on the middle of a sofa
perpendicular to the hassock. They begin talking about the war.*

VONNEGUT: Only one person came home from World War
Two who was treated like a hero and that was Audie Murphy. Everybody knew he was the only hero.

HELLER: I felt like a hero when I came home. And I still feel
like a hero when people interview me. People think it quite
remarkable that I was in combat in an airplane and I flew
sixty missions even though I tell them that the missions
were largely milk runs.

VONNEGUT: And what kind of medals did you get?

HELLER: I got the conventional medals, which came automatically. Air Medal with five or six clusters. You know, you're in my new book. Unless you object.

VONNEGUT: Good. Good.

HELLER: In that sense it's not a sequel. One of the characters does end up in Dresden and he's talking to a guy named Vonnegut. You're not in *Catch-22*, so it's not properly a sequel.

VONNEGUT: Joe, when he was working on this book earlier, wanted to get an officer or a high-ranking noncom into Dresden. You know, the guy who had done bombing. Then, finally, he's bombed, and this is technically impossible. Noncoms and officers were not allowed to work. They were kept in big stalags out in the countryside.

PLAYBOY: How did you feel when Iraq was bombed?

HELLER: I felt awful about the whole Gulf war. My feeling is that at that time Bush still hadn't figured out why he had invaded Panama, and he didn't know why he was making war in Iraq. And he still doesn't. I think it was an atrocity.

VONNEGUT: I can see where you might catch a whole lot of people and have to kill them that way, particularly from the air. But people in our war, the good war, were sickened by it afterward and would not talk about it. When we went to war, we had two fears. One was that we'd get killed. The other was that we might have to kill someone. Imagine somebody coming back from the Gulf, particularly a pilot, saying, "Gee, I'm lucky. I didn't have to kill anybody." TV has dehumanized us to the point where this is acceptable. It was like shooting up a crowd going home from a football game on a Saturday afternoon. Shoot the front vehicle and the back vehicle and then go up and down and kill everybody dead. A disgraceful way to act. In the SS—probably a tough branch of the SS and maybe just officers—they had to strangle a cat during their training. With their hands. And I think TV has done this to a whole lot of people without anybody's having to strangle a cat.

HELLER: I would guess that after one strangled the first cat, the rest are easier. The next five or six are pure fun. Then it becomes a kind of pastime. A careless hobby. Like lighting a cigarette.

PLAYBOY: Why do we celebrate war with a parade?

HELLER: I think it's dangerous to use the expression "we" in dealing with war. One of the fallacies has to do with democracy. I don't think we've had a President in my lifetime who came to the White House with a significant proportion of the eligible voters voting.

VONNEGUT: Yeah, but you got at least one great President, didn't you?

HELLER: Which one?

VONNEGUT: Roosevelt.

HELLER: I often wonder, if I were an adult in Roosevelt's time, whether I would have revered him and loved him the way I do in retrospect.

VONNEGUT: The Russians loved the czar as long as they could. Right up until the last minute, because he was the father.

HELLER: Once the war broke out, I think everyone wanted it over quickly and did not want to see a U.S. defeat. There was so much bunkum and deception.

PLAYBOY: Instead of killing several hundred thousand Iraqis, why wasn't Saddam Hussein "disappeared"?

HELLER: It's not that easy. I think they were bombing places selectively in the hope of getting him. The way they missed Qaddafi and got his daughter.

VONNEGUT: There's a wonderful documentary Canadians made when people were really sick of the war—World War Two, that is. People were dying in industrial quantities. Fifty thousand nameless guys going over the top and they focused on these romantic figures up there in the airplanes and revived interest in the war.

HELLER: Is this in the U.S. or France?

VONNEGUT: All fighter pilots. Everybody loved Von Rich-thofen as much as anybody else. It was, "Who was going to get him?" My agent, incidentally, Ken Littauer, who is dead now, was Lieutenant Colonel Littauer, who in military history was the first man to strafe a trench. He was a full colonel at the age of twenty-two and he and Rickenbacker and Nordoff and Hall were all in the Lafayette Flying Corps. They were the only guys in the American Air Force who really knew how to fly and fight. Littauer was supposed to be just an observation guy, out for artillery. He decided, "What the hell! The object is to kill people." And he peeled off and I guess he had a machine gun.

HELLER: It was fun in the beginning. We were kids, nine-teen, twenty years old, and had real machine guns in our hands. Not those things at the penny arcades at Coney Island. You got the feeling that there was something glorious about it. Glorious excitement. The first time I saw a plane on fire and parachutes coming down, I looked at it with a big grin on my face. I was disappointed in those early missions of mine where nobody shot at us.

VONNEGUT: Morley Safer wrote about going in after B-52s dropped these enormous bombs on an area suspected of sheltering Viet Cong. He said the smell was terrible, there were parts of human bodies hanging in treetops. The poor pilots don't usually see that.

HELLER: Air Force people don't see it. I didn't realize until I read Paul Fussel's book on World War One that almost everybody who took my artillery shell or bombing grenade was going to be dismembered, mutilated. Not the way it is in the movies where somebody gets hit, clutches his chest and falls down dead. They are blown apart. Blown into pieces.

PLAYBOY: Is there a hidden agenda behind our romance with war?

HELLER: American rulers are discovering that the way to get instant popularity is to go to war. I think if the Vietnam war had been over in a month or two, Johnson might still be President—and might still be alive.

PLAYBOY: Do you think there's a relationship between the CIA and the war?

VONNEGUT: I know Allen Ginsberg made a bet with Richard Helms, who was the head of the CIA. When the Vietnam war was going on, Allen bet him his little bronze dumbbell or some sacred object that the CIA was in the drug business and it would come out sooner or later. Flying drugs in and out of East Asia. I don't know whether Allen won the bet or what Helms was supposed to have given him, but I'm sure it's true.

HELLER: There's one thing about being involved in a drug trade. There's another thing about being the drug trade.

PLAYBOY: Were we in Iraq and concentrating on foreign affairs to cover up problems at home?

HELLER: Doing this last novel of mine, I find that Thucydides filed the same charge against Pericles in the war against Sparta—to divert attention from allegations of personal scandal. It's so much easier than administering your country. It's also extremely dangerous because of the temptation in a democracy.

VONNEGUT: It's also very bad if the enemy shoots back.

HELLER: Well, you have to pick enemies that won't. During the Spanish-American War, American casualties at Manila Bay were four or seven. Panama was instructive to me because such a high percentage of the number of people who went were either killed or wounded.

VONNEGUT: What was that island we attacked before, with that long runway?

HELLER: Grenada.

VONNEGUT: Some of the first guys we lost were SEALs. Because they were dropped into the ocean and never heard of again. Nobody knows what the hell happened to them.

PLAYBOY: Let's switch to censorship. Are you at all concerned about the government's intrusion into our privacy?

HELLER: Do I think, for example, this guy Pee-wee Herman should be arrested for playing with himself in an adult theater?

VONNEGUT: Did he play to climax? I really haven't kept up with the news as I should.

HELLER: But is that a crime? I would say no.

VONNEGUT: I agree with Joe.

HELLER: We may have an aversion to the idea of somebody's masturbating in a theater or in a bathroom but so long as he didn't call attention to himself—that's what we call exhibitionism.

VONNEGUT: This is a huge country. There are primitive tribes here and there who have customs and moral standards of their own. It's the way I feel about religious fundamentalists. They really ought to have a reservation. They have a right to their culture and I can see where the First Amendment would be very painful for them. The First Amendment is a tragic amendment because everyone is going to have his or her feelings hurt and your government is not here to protect you from having your feelings hurt.

PLAYBOY: What about the hurt being done to women deprived of the freedom of choice?

VONNEGUT: I think Bush is utterly insincere on the abortion issue. He probably feels about it the way most Yale graduates do. There's just political capital in pretending to be concerned about abortion. He doesn't want to push it any harder than he has to because he'd lose a big part of the electorate.

HELLER: Even if he's pretending. I'm going to quote from the introduction of *Mother Night*, "We are what we pretend to be." If those people in government are only pretending to object to sex displays or abortion, the effect is the same as if they were sincere.

PLAYBOY: Do you think Senator Helms is pretending?

VONNEGUT: Yes. There are several famous hypocrites in the South and he's surely one of them. Like the Bible thumpers. To attract a crowd.

PLAYBOY: Do you see him as a real threat?

VONNEGUT: He has a good many Christian fundamentalist followers. So he is, in fact, serving his constituents—and they are not hypocrites, I would say. But in that little railroad car that runs under Congress, I rode with a guy who worked for Helms, one of his assistants. This guy was as hip and sane and liberal as anyone. He simply had a job to do.

PLAYBOY: Let's turn to books. Are you alarmed about the corporate role in publishing?

HELLER: "Alarmed" is a strong word. I'm aware of it and I don't think the effects will be beneficial toward literature. As I get older, I begin thinking that not only are certain things inevitable, everything is inevitable.

PLAYBOY: How about censorship in publishing? What about when Simon and Schuster decided not to publish a book it had contracted for—Bret Easton Ellis' *American Psycho*—because of pressure?

HELLER: The allegation was made that the decision came from the head of Paramount which owns Simon and Schuster. But the book was published. I don't think censorship is a widespread threat in this country.

VONNEGUT: You can publish yourself. During the McCarthy era, Howard Fast published *Spartacus*. Sold it to the movies. Nobody would publish him because he was a Communist.

PLAYBOY: Are writers supportive of one another or resentful?

VONNEGUT: Writers aren't envious of one another.

HELLER: We may be envious of the success but not of one another.

VONNEGUT: Painters and poets can be deeply upset by the good luck of a colleague. Writers and novelists really don't seem to give a damn.

PLAYBOY: Are nonfiction writers more jealous and envious of one another than novelists?

VONNEGUT: I know one very close friendship that ended when one guy was working on a book and his best friend came in right behind him.

PLAYBOY: Is it more difficult to get blurbs for nonfiction than fiction because of jealousy?

VONNEGUT: Blurbs are baloney. Anybody who reads a blurb is crazy. Calvin Trillin said that "anybody who gives a blurb should he required right on the jacket to reveal his relationship to the author." It's a good way to advertise. Keep your name around.

HELLER: That's one reason, but they don't advertise as voluminously as they used to do.

VONNEGUT: When Alger Hiss wrote a book—his most recent, his side of the story—I wrote a blurb for it and I was the only blurb on the book. Startling! I thought other people would be on there with me. Howard Fast or somebody. . . .

PLAYBOY: Did you ever review each other's books?

HELLER: No.

VONNEGUT: Yes. We hadn't known each other very well. And then we were neighbors out here and Joe had finally written another book.

HELLER: That was 1974.

VONNEGUT: Since *Something Happened* was only his second book, he was rather anxious to find out who was reviewing it for the *Times*.

HELLER: I'm going to correct this impression when you finish.

VONNEGUT: It wasn't unethical at the beginning of the summer because I really didn't know him that well. But I spent most of the summer writing the review and I got to see more and more of Joe. Who did they tell you was reviewing it for the *Times*? You change the story.

HELLER: I knew fairly early you were doing it because Irwin Shaw brought it out. And I said, "You never should have told me that." I knew enough about you to know that you would not undertake it unless you were going to write favorably about it. Then I began to get anxious about you and myself. Each time they got word of a good review from somewhere else, I made it a point to tell you.

VONNEGUT: Talk about disinformation.

HELLER: I didn't want you to feel inhibited in your praise.

VONNEGUT: Was there anyone who really tied a can to your tail? Anybody who really hated the book?

HELLER: There were reviewers who were disappointed, because it was not another *Catch-22* and they expected it to be.

VONNEGUT: Well, *Catch-22* was sort of a fizzle when it first came out, wasn't it?

HELLER: Despite an advertising campaign that has never been equaled or surpassed in terms of the number of ads.

VONNEGUT: Did Bertrand Russell praise the book?

HELLER: He not only praised the book, he had his secretary call me up and arrange for us to meet. It was one of the few thrilling encounters I've had in my lifetime. It's a long drive to Wales from London. Russell was already ninety. And he looked exactly like his photographs. I had that experience with Venice the first time I went to Venice. It looks exactly like Venice. Paris doesn't. London doesn't. New York doesn't. Venice looks exactly like Venice and Bertrand Russell looked exactly like Bertrand Russell.

VONNEGUT: I suppose it was the first unromantic book about the Air Force.

HELLER: I don't know about first. It's not a romantic book. It is romantic. I know the underlying sentimentality. Phillip Toynbee began a review of it with a paragraph that embarrasses me still. He begins listing the great works of satire in the English language and he puts this among them. I think he was the one who said it was the first war book in which fear and cowardice become a virtue.

PLAYBOY: So, who are the new Kurt Vonneguts or Joe Hellers?

HELLER: Oh, I don't think there has been anybody after us.

VONNEGUT: Well, we haven't seen Schwarzkopf's memoirs yet. (Laughs)

HELLER: You've got the name wrong. Scheisskopf.

VONNEGUT: I remember Schwarzkopf's father, a police commissioner in New Jersey. Then he was the host on a radio show called *Gangbusters*.

HELLER: Somebody told me his father was also the head of the regional Selective Service department in New Jersey and New York.

VONNEGUT: Four stars is a lot of stars. That's all Pershing had was four stars.

HELLER: They didn't have five stars then. Five stars was not a rank in World War Two.

PLAYBOY: I had a little trouble when he said that being under a missile attack was no more dangerous than being in a thunderstorm.

VONNEGUT: His comment on the Scud, I think, was that shooting down a Scud was like shooting down a Goodyear blimp, because these things are not very fast or hard to hit. There was a story in World War Two about a Dutch cruiser that escaped from the Nazis just as they were occupying Holland. The ship pulled into a fiord somewhere and put on war paint, purple and green stripes, and sailed into the Firth of Clyde, where the British navy was anchored in Scotland, and the skipper of the cruiser called to the flagship and asked, "How do you like our new camouflage?" And the answer that came back was "Where are you?"

PLAYBOY: Is that true?

HELLER: Would Vonnegut joke?

PLAYBOY: Do either of you read any contemporary writers?

VONNEGUT: Well, it's not like the medical profession where you have to find out the latest treatments. I've been reading Nietzsche.

HELLER: And I've been reading Thomas Mann. I hesitate because maybe I'm reading more difficult books to grasp than nonfiction. Scientific books. Philosophy, I would not be able to read rapidly. I have a definite impression that I'm reading more slowly than I used to.

VONNEGUT: There's no urgency about reading anymore. We're not trying to keep up. I have that big book by Mark Helprin and I don't think I'm going to read it because I'm too lazy.

PLAYBOY: What about Norman Mailer's?

VONNEGUT: That's none of your business. Norman's a friend of mine.

HELLER: I intend to read it at one sitting. I read contemporary writers.

PLAYBOY: Such as whom?

HELLER: It wouldn't be "whom." It would be a particular work. If the work is described in a way I feel would be interesting to me. Not enjoyable. Interesting. I look into every galley I'm sent. I don't have time to read them. Just the way I don't get as many invitations to parties as Kurt Vonnegut does.

VONNEGUT: They've stopped coming. Well, I'm reading Martin Amis.

HELLER: The last book?

VONNEGUT: It's a new one. The whole thing runs backward. Time runs backward. It's very hard to follow.

HELLER: I will read Julian Barnes's new novel. I like Julian Barnes for reasons I can't explain.

PLAYBOY: Any women?

HELLER: You have to name some.

PLAYBOY: Ann Beattie.

HELLER: I've read Ann Beattie.

VONNEGUT: I read Margaret Atwood's *The Handmaid's Tale* and thought it was terrific. I wrote her a fan letter. Joe said one time in an interview or somewhere that people in advertising are better read and wittier than most novelists.

HELLER: And most academics. That was my experience when *Catch-22* came out.

PLAYBOY: What is your favorite book of Joe's?

VONNEGUT: He hasn't written enough to choose from.

HELLER: There's no answer that would be convincing and satisfying.

VONNEGUT: You know about the frog-and-peach restaurant? Well, there are four things on the menu. You can have a frog. You can have a peach. You can have a frog stuffed with a peach or a peach stuffed with a frog. When you ask what is my favorite of Heller's, you don't have a very long menu. I have gone the extra mile with Joe. I have seen *We Bombed in New Haven* performed at Yale. Not many people can say that.

HELLER: More at Yale than on Broadway. I used to think *Catch-22* was my best novel until I read Kurt's review of *Something Happened*. Now I think *Something Happened* is.

PLAYBOY: What is your favorite book of Kurt's?

HELLER: Oh, I don't like any of his works. I just give blurbs to his books so we can remain friends.

VONNEGUT: I'm sure Joe doesn't mind this being discussed. It takes him a while to write a book. He might be a different author in each case because he's a decade older. Nietzsche says the philosopher's view of the world makes his reputation and he doesn't change it. It reflects how old he was then. Plato's philosophy is the philosophy of a man of thirty-five.

PLAYBOY: You're writing a movie, we hear.

VONNEGUT: Yes, with Steven Wright.

HELLER: Boy, I'd love to write a movie script.

PLAYBOY: Why don't you collaborate?

HELLER: Take me as a secret collaborator? Pay me just enough to qualify for the medical plan of the Writers' Guild.

VONNEGUT: It's hack work. I just got interested in Steven Wright. He was out here and stayed with me for a couple of days. You know who he is?

HELLER: Not really.

VONNEGUT: He has sort of the build of a Woody Allen and that melancholy and he doesn't know what the hell he's going to say next. And so you're listening and finally he says it, but he never says where he is from, what he is. He is in fact a Roman Catholic. Most people assume he's Jewish. But he's very smart not to say, "I'm from Boston." He's very hot on the college circuit. He gets fifteen thousand dollars an appearance and he does fifty a year.

HELLER: Are you being paid for the screenplay?

VONNEGUT: I'm doing it on spec. But I won't show it to them until they pay me.

PLAYBOY: What about Hollywood?

HELLER: I love it. I don't work that much and I will accept every offer I get. I love going to Hollywood because I know people there. When I go there, somebody else is always paying the expenses.

VONNEGUT: How do you know people there?

HELLER: Almost every friend I had on the Island moved out there after the war. Then my nephew was out there working for Paramount TV.

PLAYBOY: Kurt, we gather you're less enthralled in dealing with Hollywood.

VONNEGUT: No. There are two novelists who should be very grateful to Hollywood. Margaret Mitchell is one and I'm the other one.

HELLER: *Thelma & Louise* is the first movie I've seen in years. I liked it. Well, a year ago I saw that Italian film *Cinema Paradiso*. I usually don't like the movies.

PLAYBOY: Did it bother you that in *Thelma & Louise* the heroines killed a man?

HELLER: No. It doesn't bother me when they kill cowboys or Indians. It's only the movies. There are so many movies where the woman turns out to be the murderess. I didn't see it as a movie with any kind of morality. It was a movie about two women who get into trouble.

PLAYBOY: Does a movie like *Thelma & Louise* indicate a change in the culture?

VONNEGUT: You have forgotten that we are so old we are contemporaries of Bonnie and Clyde and of Ma Barker. She was the head of the family. We know about some really rough women.

PLAYBOY: Bonnie still followed Clyde, didn't she?

HELLER: You're not asking us about women. You're asking us about characters in motion pictures.

PLAYBOY: At the recent St. John's rape trial in New York, one of the jurors wore a T-shirt that read, UNZIP MY FLY. What is that all about?

VONNEGUT: I don't know, but it's a very popular T-shirt.

PLAYBOY: Where is that coming from?

VONNEGUT: A T-shirt factory, obviously.

PLAYBOY: Why would someone want to wear that?

VONNEGUT: Joe and I had a publisher in England for a while and his fly was always unzipped.

PLAYBOY: Does sex get better when you're older?

HELLER: Does what?

PLAYBOY: Does it get better when you're older or not?

HELLER: I don't know. I haven't had it since I was young.

VONNEGUT: I don't know if he's kidding or not.

HELLER: Oh, I've had no sex as an adult.

VONNEGUT: He's a comedian.

PLAYBOY: Well, what about you, Kurt? Does sex get better when you get older?

VONNEGUT: You get to be a better lover.

HELLER: I find I'm much more virile now than I was.

PLAYBOY: More what?

HELLER: More potent. I want to do it more often than when I was seventeen or eighteen.

PLAYBOY: Why don't you guys write more explicitly about sex and its emotional trappings?

HELLER: More explicitly than what? You keep projecting. You keep attaching emotional reactions to sexual reactions. Earlier you used the words "love" and "sex" and now you're suggesting emotional reactions to sex. By emotional I'm sure you mean something different from the sensory responses.

PLAYBOY: Well, emotions are different from senses.

HELLER: I don't think there is a necessary correlation between emotional responses and sex.

PLAYBOY: Didn't D. H. Lawrence write about emotions?

HELLER: That was the content of his artistic or literary consciousness. I don't think writers have a choice, by the way. I think we discover a field in which we can be proficient and that's our imagination. My imagination cannot work like Kurt's and I don't think his can work like mine. Neither of us could write like Philip Roth or Norman Mailer. I know John Updike has a lot of tales of the sexual encounter. And I suppose there are writers who can do it and will do it and want to do it.

PLAYBOY: Henry Miller?

HELLER: What you get there is the raw activity.

PLAYBOY: Anaïs Nin?

VONNEGUT: I haven't read the porn she wrote. If you have an attractive man and woman coming together, the reader is going to want to see them do it or find out why they didn't do it. And so you can't talk about anything else. The example I use is Ralph Ellison's *Invisible Man*. It's about this black guy who is looking for comfort and enlightenment somewhere in American society. It's a picaresque novel. If he ever ran into a woman who really loved him and he loved her, that would be the end of the book. It would be as short as my books. And Ellison has to keep him away from women.

HELLER: I must say, for me, it doesn't normally make good literature. Fiction having extensive detail about the gymnastics of copulation or sexual congress—or even the alleged responses to it—does not make interesting reading to me. It's like trying to describe the noise of a subway train. There are people who can do it. Young writers go in for that type of description. But when they're finished, all they've done is described the noise of a subway train coming into a station or pulling out of a station. Is that the noblest objective of a work of fiction? To convince the reader that what you're writing about is really happening? I don't think so.

PLAYBOY: Isaac Bashevis Singer said, "In sex and love, human character is revealed more than anywhere else."

VONNEGUT: He is liable to say anything to be interesting. He entertains in that way. Do you know what he said about free will? "We have no choice."

HELLER: That's not been proved. I would not agree with that. The same two people could have come together sexually numerous times and it could be a different experience and the person's character doesn't change from copulation to copulation.

PLAYBOY: But one gets to know the other better with increased copulation.

HELLER: I don't think so.

VONNEGUT: Well, this is the French theory of the golden key.

HELLER: You learn more at lunch than you do in the meeting before. In phone conversation.

VONNEGUT: Nietzsche had a little one-liner on how to choose a wife. He said, "Are you willing to have a conversation with this woman for the next forty years?" That's how to pick a wife.

HELLER: If people were more widely read, there'd be fewer marriages.

VONNEGUT: I will give you all the money that's left after the divorce if you can get me a film clip of Frank Sinatra making it with Nancy Reagan. I think that is the funniest damn thing.

PLAYBOY: In the White House?

VONNEGUT: I don't care where. Those two scrawny people.

PLAYBOY: Have you read Kitty Kelley?

VONNEGUT: Sure. Parts of it. Joe gets all those books. And I just leaf through them. About the Kennedys or about any scandal.

HELLER: I didn't look at it.

PLAYBOY: Why do you think we're so interested in scandal?

VONNEGUT: Just because it's in the papers. The same way we pretend to be interested in sports, a way to say hello to a stranger. "What did you think of the second game of the World Series? What did you think of this? What do you think of the Super Bowl?" It's a way of saying hello.

HELLER: I agree with him. I have a slight, diminishing

taste for gossip and for scandal. If you're taking about the most interesting things in the newspapers, I think our news reporting is abominable. There shouldn't be daily papers. Maybe once a week they ought to publish.

VONNEGUT: John F. Kennedy was off the scale. He was a freak! I mean, he was in the *Guinness Book of Records* for the number of women he screwed, apparently.

HELLER: I would have liked him a lot more if I had known at the time what was going on.

PLAYBOY: Why is a man respected for having many sexual relationships and a woman disrespected or scorned?

HELLER: The explanation would be the terrible fears of impotency men have and the jealousy that's concomitant with that. Mark Twain says that the only reason the Bible was against adultery was to keep the woman from screwing someone else. His explanation is that a man is like a candle and he's going to burn out, and the woman is like a candlestick and she can hold a million candles.

PLAYBOY: But women also scorn women who have had many sexual experiences.

HELLER: Women with bad reputations can be attractive to a man. They are to me. But a wife or a daughter like that would be a terrible embarrassment to me.

VONNEGUT: Joe's got the Freudian explanation. I think that men can't help suspecting that women are stronger and better people than they are and they learn that from their mother. I would agree with that.

PLAYBOY: Do you think younger women are sexier than older women?

VONNEGUT: No.

HELLER: I agree with Kurt.

VONNEGUT: I taught at Iowa for a year and there were a whole lot of blondes there because of our Scandinavian population. I was not interested in these undergraduate girls at all.

HELLER: Even when I was young, I found older women more attractive than young girls.

PLAYBOY: Is there anyone for whom you lust in your heart?

VONNEGUT: My goodness!

HELLER: Madonna. Madonna.

VONNEGUT: Joe mentioned one of Artie Shaw's wives. Seemed to me the sexiest woman I ever saw was Ava Gardner.

HELLER: Kathleen Winsor was pretty hot.

VONNEGUT: Rita Hayworth. I took it hard when she came down with Alzheimer's.

PLAYBOY: Joe, were you serious about Madonna?

HELLER: No.

PLAYBOY: Who's going to win the Democratic nomination?

HELLER: I have a feeling it might be me.

PLAYBOY: You? Are you going to vote for yourself?

VONNEGUT: He will have to register first.

HELLER: I'd register and I'd pose. I would if I ran.

PLAYBOY: Kurt, would you vote for Joe?

VONNEGUT: Certainly. It's a figurehead job in any case.

HELLER: I'd run on two issues. And I believe I'd win. The first would be, as President of the federal government, I would take no steps whatsoever to interfere with a woman's right to terminate a pregnancy. The second is I would find some way to institute a national health program in this country. Don't ask me where the money's going to come from, I will find a way to do it.

VONNEGUT: The big difference between conservatives and liberals is that killing doesn't seem to bother the conservatives at all. The liberals are chickenhearted about people dying. Conservatives thought that the massacre, the killing, of so many people in Panama was OK. I think they're really Darwinians. It's all right that people are starving to death on the streets because that's the nature of work.

HELLER: Western civilization has made a pact with the Devil. I think the story of Faust has to do with Western civilization. You might say white civilization. The Devil or God said, "I'll give you knowledge to do great things. But you're going to use that knowledge to destroy the environment and to destroy yourself." You mentioned Darwin. I think what we're experiencing now is the natural state of evolution. Half the society is underprivileged and maybe a third of the rest is barely surviving. The trouble with the Administration is that it doesn't want to deal with the problem. It doesn't want to define it as a problem because then it will have to deal with it.

THE MELANCHOLIA OF EVERYTHING COMPLETED

INTERVIEW BY JC GABEL

FIRST PUBLISHED IN *STOP SMILING*
ISSUE 27: ODE TO THE MIDWEST, AUGUST 2006

"The arts put a man at the center of the universe," Kurt Vonnegut told the graduating class of Bennington College in 1970, "whether he belongs there or not."

Growing up in Indianapolis during the Great Depression, Kurt Vonnegut Jr. did not consider the arts to be a part of anyone's universe. According to the legendary author and humorist, the arts were discouraged in his family. Vonnegut's father urged his children toward rationalism. Science was the answer, he was assured, not the arts.

Vonnegut's older brother, Bernard, a physical chemist who studied at MIT, thought technology would solve the world's problems. Partly to please his father—Kurt Vonnegut Sr., an architect whose business suffered during the Depression—his son, Kurt Jr., followed in his older brother's footsteps, studying biochemistry at Cornell University in Ithaca, New York. Yet the younger Vonnegut had already shown promise as a writer at his daily high school newspaper, the *Shortridge Daily Echo*. He later worked as a columnist, writer and assistant managing editor at the *Cornell Sun*.

Fate, of course, continued to intervene. Midway through his studies Vonnegut was failing chemistry. He enlisted in the Army and was thrust into World War II, after some training in mechanical engineering. He became a battalion scout with the 106th Infantry Division. At the Battle of the Bulge, Vonnegut was captured by the Germans, became a POW and was later taken to Dresden, where he witnessed the firebombing of that city, which killed 135,000 citizens. Vonnegut's portrayal of these events formed the basis of his most cherished novel, *Slaughterhouse-Five: Or The Children's Crusade*. The title is taken from the meat locker in which he and his fellow Allied POWs took shelter while Dresden was destroyed. Upon his return to the U.S. in 1945, he was awarded a Purple Heart.

It's now 2006, and America's greatest living fiction writer is done writing. He has seen 14 novels published (*Player Piano, The Sirens of Titan, Mother Night, Cat's Cradle, God Bless You, Mr. Rosewater, Slaughterhouse-Five, Breakfast of Champions* and *Timequake*, among them), three short-story collections (*Canary in a Cathouse, Welcome to the Monkey House* and *Bagombo Snuff Box*), a play (*Happy Birthday, Wanda June*), two books of essays and opinions (*Wampeters, Foma, and Granfalloons* and *Palm Sunday*), as well as numerous adaptations of his works for television and film.

His most recent collection of writings, *A Man Without a Country* (Seven Stories Press), is composed of short pieces, most of which he wrote for the magazine *In These Times*. When it was released in September 2005, it became an instant bestseller.

"I've lived a full life," he says. He's been an author and freelance writer now for 56 years. Some previous jobs he's held include police reporter for Chicago's City News

Bureau, PR writer for General Electric, teacher in Cape Cod, advertising copywriter and Saab manager in Barnstable, Massachusetts.

He's also taught writing at colleges, on and off, for more than 40 years, beginning at the Iowa Writers' Workshop, then Harvard, followed by the City College of New York and Smith College, in Northampton, Massachusetts.

He has a total of seven children: three of his own (Mark, Edie and Nanny), three he raised after his sister, Alice, died of cancer in 1958 (Tiger, Jim and Steven), and Lily, the daughter of Vonnegut and his second wife, author and photographer Jill Krementz. More than half of them are professional artists in one form or another. It turns out, art does run in the Vonnegut family.

Vonnegut has been creating art most of his life with felt-tip pens and markers. For a better part of the last 15 years, he's been creating art exclusively with Kentucky-born artist and screen-printmaker, Joe Petro III. Each piece is hand-drawn or painted by Vonnegut, and hand-printed by Petro from his studio in Lexington.

In the Author's Note to *A Man Without a Country*, Vonnegut pays tribute to Petro, his friend and collaborator, while describing more about their process: "Joe makes prints of some of [my work], one by one, color by color, by means of the time-consuming, archaic silk screen process, practiced by almost nobody else anymore: squeegeeing inks through cloths and onto paper. This process is so painstaking and tactile, almost balletic, that each print Joe makes is a painting in its own right.

"Our partnership's name, Origami Express," he contin-
ues, "is my tribute to the many-layered packages Joe makes
for prints he sends for me to sign and number."

"Everything I've done is in print," Vonnegut tells me
from his house in Long Island. "I have fulfilled my des-
tiny, such as it is, and I have nothing more to say. So now
I'm writing little things—one line here, two lines there,
sometimes a poem. I like working crossword puzzles. And I
make art. I didn't expect to live this long." He has reached,
he says, what Nietzsche called "the melancholia of everything completed."

Much to his surprise, Vonnegut has outlived Mark
Twain, a man he not only physically resembles and admires
greatly—he's called him "a national treasure"—but with
whom he also shares a comic bond. Twain died at the age
of 76 in 1910. Born in 1922, Vonnegut is now 83. Twain
amazed and entertained Americans throughout the latter
half of the 19th century; Vonnegut did the same for Americans in the latter half of the 20th century. Both men were
born writers, practiced novelists and, most important, sav-
age satirists quick with endless black humor and sharp wit.
Each managed to have the last laugh, no matter how dire
life and times got. So it goes.

*This summer, Vonnegut and I talked by phone six or seven times,
from the middle of June to the middle of July. The following
interview is a portion of those conversations.*

STOP SMILING: Tell me about the American Midwest you

remember from childhood, and the one you came back to, after WWII.

KURT VONNEGUT: I was born in Indianapolis, but I'm a Chicagoan who lives in New York. I went to the University of Chicago. I worked for Chicago's City News Bureau as a street reporter, and my first child, Mark, was born there.

SS: Do you think the Midwest is a good place to grow up?

KV: If George W. Bush got mad enough at me and exiled me back to Indianapolis, I could make a decent life there. I could hack it in Indianapolis.

SS: In your last book, *A Man Without a Country*, there is a story about Germans moving to America. You wrote that your pioneering relatives came to the New World more because they were attracted to the Constitution than because they were being oppressed.

KV: I've said in my book that the Statue of Liberty was calling for the people in awful shape. And of course they arrived. The country was welcoming everybody. They were educated German gentiles and Jews as well. They were savvy in business and learned English, and were in a good shape to establish themselves, which they did. This raised a feeling which I still sense sometimes when face to face with an Anglo—it raised the question: Who the hell's country is this anyway? All the businesses in Indianapolis were largely taken over by Germans—again German Jews and gentiles alike.

SS: You always talk about the importance of extended families. Do you get together with your own very often?

KV: It's hard to do. We're dispersed. I want people to have extended families, but economic realities disperse us. I had an extended family in Indianapolis. I think there were 32 of them in the phone book at one time. None of my kids are in Indianapolis.

SS: You and your family long ago gravitated East. What is your theory about fresh water people versus salt-water people?

KV: When my ancestors arrived, they were thunderstruck by all this land. They were right in the middle of it. Arable land stretched out for hundreds of miles in all directions. So the land, the continent, was enough to think about. New York and San Francisco and West Coast people are oceanic and feel very close to Europe or to Asia, and the people in the Middle West are continental. One is not better than the other. It just happens to be an interesting difference. Where did you grow up?

SS: Illinois.

KV: All right. You're a fresh water person.

SS: Did studying anthropology at the University of Chicago lead you to become an atheist?

KV: No. I'm descended from boatloads of Germans who arrived about the time of the Civil War. They were so called "free thinkers." They were educated people who decided that the priest or the preacher didn't know what he was talking about when it came to the origin of things. It was largely influenced by Darwin. They formed clubs and picnics, calling themselves free thinkers. But in two World Wars, German-Americans were so hated and the free thinkers were so specifically German, they stopped calling themselves that. I take part in my hereditary religion, which is what is called a humanist. I am honorary president of the American Humanist Association. At the same time, I do not remotely proselytize and my particular war buddy who is dead now— his name is Bernard O'Hare and appears in several of my books—gave up on God after the War. He gave up being a Roman Catholic. I thought that was too much to lose. I didn't want him to do that.

SS: After finishing at U of C, you went right to Chicago's News Bureau and became a journalist professionally. Did you have some experience working for newspapers in high school and college?

KV: Yes. I had to find some way to make a living. I already had a kid, for God's sake, and I had just been discharged. I got married and my wife got pregnant immediately in

Chicago. I didn't have a clue as to how the hell I was going to make a living. Anthropology is surely no way to do it, unless you have a Ph.D. I went to an overachiever's high school in Indianapolis, which no longer exists. It was called Shortridge High School, and since 1906, it had a daily newspaper. I was an editor at the Shortridge *Daily Echo*, and I learned to write. It was beneficial, really, because it made me aware immediately of the response of readers. You publish something people don't like and you hear about it right away.

I knew how to paste up a front page and write headlines. At the City News Bureau, we phoned in our stories and we phoned in leads. The first thing you'd say is who, what, when, where and why. In writing fiction, that's what I always did. I made sure the reader knew at once where he was, too. Fiction is a game for two. You have to make it possible for a reader to play along. I have taught creative writing at Harvard, City College of New York, the Iowa Writers' Workshop and, most recently, at Smith College. Nowadays, a student will withhold a crucial piece of information for the sake of surprise later in the story—only on page 18 do you find out this person is blind; only on page 15 do you find out that this is actually happening in 1850. The reader doesn't enjoy that.

SS: You've always said that certain people are born writers. Have you always wanted to write?

KV: My brother was 10 years older than me. Bernard

Vonnegut, Ph.D. from MIT in physical chemistry. He thought science was the answer to everything, and he thought the arts were ornamental. He would talk about a dumb uncle of ours who did nothing but read novels. Art was absolutely taboo for me growing up. My father was quite beat down by the Depression. My big brother Bernie said it was a waste of money if they sent me to college, unless I studied chemistry. So that was what I did at Cornell. I was also on the *Cornell Daily Sun*, which was Ithaca, New York's morning paper. I became assistant managing editor. I would have been managing editor, but I went to war instead.

I was flunking chemistry and hating it. I was bored stiff by it, and robbing other people of their liberal arts educations. We'd talk about all kinds of interesting stuff. They'd tell me what books to read and so forth. When I went to war after three years of college, I was practically flunking everything: physics, math, all of it—barely passing. I went to the war and the Army sent me back to college. It's the reason I wasn't an officer—the officer's candidate school was closed. They had plenty of people willing to be saluted, so they took all us college kids and sent us back to college with no chance of promotion. I flunked thermodynamics twice—once at Carnegie Mellon, which used to be called Carnegie Tech, and again at the University of Tennessee. What they wanted when we successfully invaded Europe was a whole lot of riflemen to sweep across the continent. So that's what I was. I never had an opportunity to get a promotion. The things I saw as a private—

I wouldn't miss it for anything.

SS: Did fighting the war make you want to go to school for anthropology, perhaps to learn and maybe write about other cultures of the world, after having witnessed so much death and destruction?

KV: I was still cowed by the science thing. Actually, anthropology calls itself a science. It turns out it isn't. It's a form of autobiography. We all had to take a course in the anthropology department, which everybody should take. It's called "Peoples of the World," and it is a study of society after society, based on the writings of explorers, missionaries and imperialists of all different kinds. It was quite wonderful to see the varieties of culture and realize their inventions. That was helpful.

SS: In the last few years you've been writing—mostly nonfiction—for the small Chicago magazine *In These Times*. I'm curious how that relationship came about?

KV: I don't know. I turned 80, and nobody paid any attention. Then this paper out in the Midwest—Chicago, my spiritual hometown—said, "Hey, how are you? Why don't you write something for us?" I thought that was nice. I went on writing for them. I had sent out op-ed pieces to the *New York Times* again and again and again, and they would never print them.

SS: Why do you think?

KV: Because [the editorials] stunk, probably.

SS: You wrote a piece for *In These Times* that dealt with the death of one of your most cherished characters. Did you kill off Kilgore Trout, or will we see him again?

KV: Oh no. I'm all through writing except for poems and shorts, and I do art.

SS: You've been drawing for four or five decades. But in the last decade you've been working with Joe Petro III, who's from Lexington, Kentucky, on dozens of art-related projects. How did this come about?

KV: As I said, art was taboo when I was growing up. My father was full of self-pity. He was an architect. I would have liked to be an architect, but I believed my brother. My impulse was to make art anyway. Here I am. It was a wonderful break. Joe Petro said, "Why don't we work together?" It was a wonderful thing to happen to me at the end of my life.

There's a woman's college in Lexington called Midway, and I spoke there once. Speaking was a big part of my business life. Mark Twain made more money speaking than he did from writing. Anyway, I did about six speeches in the fall and six in the spring. I quit that now. I was invited to Midway, and Joe Petro was there. He said, "Why don't you do a self-portrait? I'll make a silk-screen of it and we'll use it as a poster." So I did it. I got out there and I saw what he can do. He's an artist, too. He was a zoology major in college. He does these beautifully detailed accurate pictures of nature for Greenpeace. Anyway, after I did the self-portrait he said, "Why don't we keep going?" And so we did. It was a very welcome invitation.

It was without any expectation of doing anything with the picture. Joe Petro got me drawing commercially. Putting it on the web, making silk-screens based on drawings by me. If it hadn't been for Joe, I wouldn't be doing it now. So Joe made this happen and as I've said about him, he did the most wonderful thing for me—he gave me a job.

I realized something this morning at the Museum of Modern Art, where they were having a press reception before the opening of their Dada show. Marcel Duchamp, Max Ernst and all those guys started making these very strange works of art after the First World War. Duchamp famously signed a urinal "R. Mutt." Anyway, I saw that urinal this morning and I realized that's what Joe and I are doing—Dada. Dada was the artists' response to the senselessness of the First World War. Who wants to make a picture of noble human beings? Joe and I are practicing Dada now. They were protesting the meaninglessness in life.

ss: Would you say you wanted to be a painter more than a writer?

kv: I wanted to be an architect like my father, and, like a lot of architects, I also expected to paint. Before ever meeting Joe, I had done art one way or another. I made paintings, although not with any regularity. There's nothing new about making pictures. My father painted, particularly when his architecture business failed during the Great Depression. There were art materials all over the house, and my late sister, Alice, was a wonderful sculptor. She got off a great line: "Just because you have talent doesn't mean you have to do something with it."

When I used to be a speaker at colleges, I'd say, "Look, practice an art, no matter how badly or how well you do it. It will make your soul grow." That's why you do it. You don't do it to become famous or rich. You do it to make your soul grow. This would include singing in the shower, dancing to the radio by yourself, drawing a picture of your roommate or writing a poem or whatever. Please practice an art. Have the experience of becoming. It's so sad that many public school systems are eliminating the arts because it's no way to make a living. What's important is to have the experience of becoming, which is as necessary as food or sex. It's really quite a sensation—to become.

The trouble I've had with art criticism is that it discourages people from painting. Dance criticism discourages people from dancing. But hell, everyone ought to be painting. It's such a pleasant thing to do. With critics, it has to be original, as though the arts were like science, where you make progress. Hell, there's no need to make progress. I'm kind of a cubist. More than anybody else I've ripped off Paul Klee.

The power of the museums is to say, "This is important." The whole idea of picture framing, which is a big industry, is, "This you must look at." You've taken a piece of the world and you've isolated it in a frame and it must be looked at, which is nice. But here we've got a big Dada show going on in the Museum of Modern Art and you must look at *this*. I'm wandering around all of New York and looking at this, looking at that. Maybe not looking at anything, but when you get into a museum, you gotta look at this. The arts are a practical joke. Artists are practical jokers. They're making people respond emotionally when nothing is really going on. Which is fine. That is safe sex.

But Dada was a response to how ugly modern life had become, particularly World War I. These guys simply made pictures and works of art about themselves and not about life at all. Painters used to make noble pictures of other people and buildings and scenes, and World War I was so shocking and made life so ugly that they made pictures of nothing. Essentially, the Abstract Expressionists—most stridently Jackson Pollack, who put a canvas on his garage floor and threw paint at it. This man was perfectly capable of painting a picture of Jesus on the cross or George Washington crossing the Delaware or a field of lilies. But there's nothing noble to make a picture of anymore. The joke about art, really, is that if you frame something, people will look at it. It's a form of meditation. We're making pictures. That's all. We can make any kind of picture we want. It was true of Mondrian. It was true of Jackson Pollack. Just because there is no market for them is no reason to stop making them.

ss: Did you know Jackson Pollack?

KV: I met him briefly and wrote a piece about him for *Esquire* magazine, where they called him "Jack the Dripper." People said, "Please. Paint a pretty baby, paint a beautiful woman, a noble human being, a great horse. Is that all a painter can do? Throw paint at a canvas on his garage floor?" He was quite disgusted with what art had become. So are Joe and I. And it's fun. The function of painting—Joe's and my pictures—they're for people's homes, not a big deal in a museum. Somebody might enjoy having one in their home or office. We're not breaking new ground.

ss: Do you think there's too much emphasis on making money—not so much that there is a de-emphasis on art?

KV: Yes, and we have some of the worst schools in the world.

ss: Because of the lack of curriculum? Class size?

KV: The classes are too big. My definition of a utopia is very simple: classes of 15 or smaller—out of this, a great nation can be built. Classes have 35 students, for Christ's sake. The class ideally should be a family. Let's take care of each other. There's a person who can't get the hang of calculus? Someone should say, "Here, let me show you." A class of 35? Poor teacher.

ss: You taught writing for years. When you came across

a talented student, were you dumbfounded about what to tell them to do with their talent?

KV: I'm dumbfounded about what happened to my country. But as I say regularly in lectures, you practice an art to make your soul grow, not to make a career, be famous or be rich. It's the process of becoming. It's as essential to the growing up process as food, sex or physical exercise. You find out who you are that way. I used to challenge audiences, but I don't face them much anymore. I'd say, "Write a poem tonight. Make it as good as you possibly can. Four, six or eight lines. Make it as good as you can. Don't tell anybody what you're doing. Don't show it to anybody. When you're satisfied it's as good as you can make it, tear it up in small pieces and scatter those pieces between widely separated trash receptacles and you will find out you have received your full reward for having done it." It's the act of creation, which is so satisfying.

SS: How did you get into short-story writing for periodicals?

KV: It was such a tempting business, such a booming business with the magazines, that I could easily quit my job with General Electric and make a hell of a lot more money. *Collier's* and *Saturday Evening Post* each needed five short stories every week. There were lots of guys like me who were making good pay. A hell of a lot more than General Electric was paying.

SS: Was that strange to you? That you could write stories at home and make more money than you could working a straight job?

KV: No, not at all. It's a special skill. It's not something that anybody can do. I had the gift for writing short stories. Most people don't. Most people aren't high jumpers or pole vaulters either. It was something I could do. With my particular gift, I could move my family to Cape Cod.

SS: You always used to say that you were in the joke-making business. Do you still feel that way?

KV: Yes. I appreciate other people's jokes, too. There are some lovely things that are happening, even as the world ends. There's a wonderful new movie, Garrison Keillor's *A Prairie Home Companion*. There are great country jokes in it. God, there's a knock out. I love country jokes: "Did you try that new toilet brush I gave you?" "Yeah, but I still prefer paper."

SS: At one point, Robert Altman was talking about doing a film with one of your books—*Breakfast of Champions*.

KV: Somehow we never got together. I'm a huge fan of his, and I guess he likes what I do. But Nashville is his masterpiece.

SS: His most famous film was *MASH*, a film about finding humor during wartime. After the bleakness of the Depression and WWII, the 1950s seemed to offer people hope and now it's gone. What do you think got us here?

KV: This is a very rich country, an economic paradise, thanks to plentiful rainfall and topsoil. We could afford schools with classes of 15 or fewer and we could afford a national health plan like Norway or like Canada. Our so-called leadership brought us here.

SS: You've said that the lesson we learned from our engagement in the Vietnam War is that we found out how ruthless our leadership could be. How do you feel about that subject today?

KV: It's a calamity. That's all. This isn't the first battle I've lost. This isn't the country I'd hoped it could be, and which in fact could have been, except for a few people who feel they're entitled to own everything. What's going on now, we have wrecked the planet as a life support system, so it will slowly die. We are in a state of denial now. It would be too hard to fix it, and too expensive. There is only one party, which is People with Money. Some of them say they're Democrats and they fight with the Republicans. What everybody is saying now is we can't fix it. Just don't spoil the party. We'll keep having fun with cars as long as we can get ahold of gasoline. The weather is going to get worse and worse. More and more species are dying. In my last book, *A Man Without a Country*, I wrote a poem. I think it's an important poem. But there is no such thing as an important poem these days—nobody pays any attention. We're goners, because it would be too hard to repair it. Everybody is saying, "All right. I've only got a few more years and I'll be out of here." One of the works of art I did is a sign. It says, "Dear Future Generations: Please accept our apology." It's the most fun human beings have ever had. If you could look back at history, nobody was having any fun. Suddenly with cars, everybody started having fun. That's going to end. I won't give a shit because I'll be dead. I won't feel anything. I've tried so hard to die by natural causes, with no luck at all.

SS: What gets you up in the morning?

KV: Sunlight. The news is perfectly terrible, so we all just entertain each other.

SS: We're amusing ourselves to death?

KV: Yes. Well, there's nothing else to do, because we can't defend ourselves now against the collapse of the planet, of the life support system. I don't know what the fuck to do. Certainly windmills aren't enough. "Science is going to take care of everything. Don't worry—meanwhile, use all the gas you want." Christ, we have billionaires now. That is a huge amount of money.

SS: How can anyone be fine, even these very rich people, if the planet itself eventually dies?

KV: Because they're psychopaths. They have no conscience. They were born without a conscience. They're psychopathic personalities. There is a wonderful medical book about them. It's called *The Mask of Sanity*. It's by Dr. Hervey M. Cleckley. It's about people who were born without consciences. They don't care what happens next. They rise high in business because they're so decisive. You and I would say, "Jeez. I don't know what the hell we're going to do now." A psychopath would say, "Here's what we're going to do. Bang." Women go for these guys, too, because they're so decisive. One thing that's really scary about them—and this would be true of Bush and Cheney—is that they don't give a shit what happens to them. You could count on a guy saving his own ass. These guys don't do it. They love to succeed, but they don't care what happens to them, either.

SS: There's no way these people can be re-elected in the next election cycle.

KV: I don't care. We have no opposition party. We have only one party, and that's winners. It's people with money, and so they pretend to fight and argue back and forth.

SS: Before September 11th, it seemed like Ralph Nader's 2000 presidential run might have been a viable movement to form a third party.

KV: Television, which is owned by the fascist corporations, did not take Nader seriously. They made him appear like a fool. That's the end of any new party he wants to start. It's the same with Howard Dean. He's not taken seriously at all. I went to anti-war protests before the Iraq war began and we got absolutely no coverage. We were perfectly respectable people—men wearing jackets and ties, educated. They were solid members of the community, and no coverage at all.

During the Vietnam War protests, the government would send people to pretend to be part of us, and they were the ones who would actually raise hell. We had one rally in Washington near the Monument. I think it was Nixon's second inauguration. We were behaving ourselves. A bunch of young guys showed up who looked like athletes. They had aerosol cans and they went up to the Washington Monument and wrote "shit" and "fuck" on it. They were sent by the government. I'm sure people thought they were us.

SS: Nixon got what was coming to him. I feel like this current administration makes Nixon look like he was playing beanbag.

KV: Oh yeah. I wish Nixon were president right now. I could at least talk to him.

SS: He seemed like he was battling his own personal demons, not those of Jesus Christ and the neocon establishment.

KV: They're not Christians either. They're simply using Jesus to mobilize a group they can count on for votes. The fact that the religious right is so strong is a function of how lonely people are in this society. We all need extended families, which is what human beings have always had until very recent times—until the Industrial Revolution. We need extended families as much as we need vitamin C. You move to a new area all by yourself or with your little family, and by God there is a church there and all kinds of stuff is going on there. Sometimes there are swimming pools and gyms. People will do anything to stop being lonely—just as people will do anything to stop from suffocating. Once you join one of those families, you have fun there. It's some place to go and a lot of people to talk to, march, protest. That is the great American disease, which is so easily exploited by cynical people. It's loneliness. It is unbearable.

SS: It would be another thing if the loneliness these people felt were not being cured by religion alone, but also by art and music and dancing and freethinking.

KV: Yes, because there's a whole lot of fun. There's singing, too. Sure. I say we need extended families. We can't have them any more. It's too bad. People will join any group nearby to have a gang. I would too, if I were that lonesome. All you can do is not spoil the party. The dying of the planet is irreversible. I made up a bumper sticker a while ago. I don't have any left, but it was popular for a while. It said, "Good Earth. We could have saved it, but we were too damn cheap and lazy." We really are going to lose it. The most sensible thing to do is have fun. There's nothing we can do to stop the process. It would be too expensive and take too much time.

SS: In 2000, a fire destroyed most of your early drafts and stories, and scores of your letters. Did that crush you?

KV: It doesn't matter. I'm sick of possessions. I'm completely in print and I don't want to say any more. I've said everything I want to say, and I'm embarrassed to have lived this long. I so envy Joseph Heller and George Plimpton and all these other friends of mine who are pushing up daisies. They don't have to hear the news. That's what I want to do. I think I'd do a swell job. The only thing that disappeared in the fire here that I really miss is my master's degree from the University of Chicago.

SS: Growing up your family owned a hardware store; therefore, you had some knowledge of science, even from hammers and ten-penny nails. But it was technology that led us to drop the atomic bomb. I'm curious whether the story about how the U.S. had to drop the bomb to end the war was generally accepted at the time? Were people satisfied with that justification or were people horrified by the thought?

KV: My brother was 10 years older than me—and was the ultimate technocrat—thought science was going to do everything. I'd come home from the war—after having been a prisoner of war—and was on furlough in Indianapolis, and my brother was there. We got up one morning and there was the *Indianapolis Star* on the front doorstep, which said, "USA Bombs Japs." My brother was utterly sickened. Science was going to make everything better—so much easier, so much more fun—and this totally sickened him. It hit him in the gut. I really had no idea how horrible the news was, except through his reaction.

When he was on his deathbed, he said this again. He lived in Albany in a hospice where he was allowed to keep his cat. He had a lot of things to say on his deathbed. One of them was that he thought scientists made terrible husbands. There's another one: "If the superpowers decide to duke it out with silver iodide, I think I can live with that." Bernard discovered silver iodide. He was in on the early cloud experiments and everything. He sure didn't want to duke it out with nukes.

A whole lot of us were sickened. When I came home on a troop ship—we were sent home from Newport News, Virginia—I asked my war buddy, Bernie O'Hare, who would later become a district attorney, "What did you learn?" He said, "I will never believe my government again." We were supposed to be the good guys. We weren't supposed to hurt civilians, men, women and children. After all, Dresden—after the A-bombing of Japan—was 135,000 dead, more than the nukes killed in Japan combined. It turned out we were the bad guys, too.

SS: What did you make of North Korea launching missile tests on the Fourth of July?

KV: I thought it was a wonderful practical joke on George Bush.

SS: Stephen Hawking recently told an audience that we should seriously consider colonizing space, because it may be our only option to avoid future human extinction. Ironically, this is something you've written about in a fictional context.

KV: That must be a joke on his part. It's like what Bertrand Russell was saying, "We're the lunatic asylum of the universe." We can't colonize space. We haven't got the means of transportation. Human beings are obviously a terrible idea. The whole universe is supposed to be infected with us?

GOD BLESS YOU, MR. VONNEGUT

INTERVIEW BY J. RENTILLY

FIRST PUBLISHED IN *U.S. AIRWAYS MAGAZINE*
JUNE 2007

Kurt Vonnegut was doing the Lord's work, whether you
believe in God or not, and Vonnegut didn't. In more than
a dozen books, including *Slaughterhouse-Five*, *Cat's Cradle*,
Mother Night, and *Timequake*, the Great American Author—arguably *the* Great American Author—combined
gallows humor, satire, and science-fiction with a deep and
abiding humanism. Precious few authors have ever loved
mankind so completely and unromantically; Vonnegut saw
us for who we really are, and loved us anyway. His work,
unflinchingly brutal at times, hilariously brittle, wildly
imaginative, and always easy to read, sometimes even dot-
ted with crude line-drawings, implored us to smile on our
brothers and love one another right now, to be kind and
decent and honest and, gulp, even noble. Vonnegut always
asked us to be the very best we could be, and refused to give
up his stranglehold on our funny bone along the way. These
are things for which we should all be grateful. Each of the
four conversations this author shared with Vonnegut between October 2000 and March 6, 2007, one month before
Vonnegut's passing at the age of 84, virtually teemed with
the subject of gratitude. Jazz, fatherhood, dancing, sacrifice,
comedy, ordinary heroes, friendship and brotherhood, the
creative process, these were all things for which Vonnegut

counted as great blessings in his life, punctuated often with a hacksaw laugh, each moment expressed with a vaudevillian's sense of timing and the heart of a teacher. It is perhaps instructive that a man can fight in World War II, survive the infamous Dresden bombing, the loss of friends, wives, and countless loved ones, not to mention the last two decades of American history and still believe that "everything was beautiful and nothing hurt," which he etched onto an illustration of a tombstone, probably laughing all the while. God Bless You, Mr. Vonnegut, wherever you are, and thank you for everything.

Tell me the reasons you've been drawn to a life of creation, whether as a writer or an artist.

I've been drawing all my life, just as a hobby, without really having shows or anything. It's just an agreeable thing to do, and I recommend it to everybody. I always say to people, practice an art, no matter how well or badly, because then you have the experience of becoming and it makes your soul grow. That includes singing, dancing, writing, drawing, playing a musical instrument. What I hate about school committees today is that they cut arts programs out of the program because they say the arts aren't a way to make a living. Well, there are lots of things worth doing that are no way to make a living. (Laughs) They *are* agreeable ways to make a more agreeable life. I am having some success with pictures now because I'm well known. People would have no interest in them otherwise, and that's all right. I made them simply for the pleasure of creation. I speak with real painters and real artists from time to time about when they get their rocks off, and it's the process of actually doing it. The rest of it—rave reviews or flops, or whatever—is just noise to them. It's the doing that matters, the *becoming*. The rest of it doesn't really matter.

In the process of your becoming, you've given the world much warmth and humor. That matters, doesn't it?

I asked my son Mark what he thought life was all about, and he said, "We are here to help each other get through this thing, whatever it is." I think that says it best. You can do that—as a comedian, a writer, a painter, a musician. He's a pediatrician. There are all kinds of ways we can help each other get through today. There are some things that help. Musicians really do it for me. I wish I was one, because they help a lot. They help us get through a couple hours.

When did the art become important to you, something you practiced regularly.

My grandfather, Bernard Vonnegut, was an Indianapolis architect and a painter. My father was an architect and a painter. My sister was a very good sculptress. So there were artists and art supplies around the house all the time. I could fart around as much as I wanted. I didn't take it seriously. I was as unserious as Jackson Pollock, throwing a canvass on the ground and messing it up in the most beautiful ways.

"A lack of seriousness," you wrote, "has led to all sorts of wonderful insights."

Yes. The world is too serious. To get mad at a work of art—because maybe somebody, somewhere is blowing his stack over what I've done—is like getting mad at a hot fudge sundae.

Your books, on the surface, are not so serious, though they frequently deal with serious ideas and themes. Fifty years after *Slaughterhouse-Five*, people are still reading your books. Why do you think your books have such enduring appeal?

I've said it before: I write in the voice of a child. That makes me readable in high school. (Laughs)

When *Timequake* was published 10 years ago, you said you were basically retired as a writer. You've published two essay collections since then, *God Bless You, Dr. Kevorkian* and the best-selling *A Man Without A Country*. I wonder if the visual arts have become a substitute for writing in your life.

Well, it's something to do in my old age. (Laughs) As you may know, I'm suing a cigarette company because their product hasn't killed me yet.

Is it a different creative process for you, sitting down to write or picking up a paintbrush?

No. I used to teach a writer's workshop at the University of Iowa back in the '60s, and I would say at the start of every semester, "The role model for this course is Vincent Van Gogh—who sold two paintings to his brother." (Laughs) I just sit and wait to see what's inside me, and that's the case for writing or for drawing, and then out it comes. There are times when nothing comes. James Brooks, the fine abstract-expressionist, I asked him what painting was like for him, and he said, "I put the first stroke on the canvass and then the canvass has to do half the work." That's how serious painters are; they're waiting for the canvass to do half the work. (Laughs) Come on. Wake up.

Your wife, Jill Krementz, is a superb photographer. I wonder if her work has had any influence or provided inspiration for you as an artist.

No. But it's been a pretty big part of the marriage. I fell in love with her talent. (Laughs) I'm just so proud of her. As a consumer of her work, I like it so much, and she really knows what she's doing. She uses very little film. She just knows when to shoot. I asked her one time how she knew when to shoot. She told me about a photo session she was doing between a man and a woman being interesting with each other, and the moment to shoot was when the man ran out of material and no longer knew what to say. (Laughs)

We live in a very visual world today. Do words have any power left?

I was at a symposium some years back with my friends Joseph Heller and William Styron, both dead now, and we were talking about the death of the novel and the death of poetry, and Styron pointed out that the novel has always been an elitist art form. It's an art form for very few people, because only a few can read very well. I've said that to open a novel is to arrive in a music hall and be handed a viola. You have to perform. (Laughs) To stare at horizontal lines of phonetic symbols and Arabic numbers and to be able to put a show on in your head, it requires the reader to perform. If you can do it, you can go whaling in the South Pacific with Herman Melville or you can watch Madame Bovary make a mess of her life in Paris. All you have to do is sit there and look at a picture or a movie, and it happens to you.

Many years ago, you said that a writer's job is to use the time of a stranger in such a way that he or she will not feel the time was wasted. There are a lot of ways for a stranger to pass time these days.

That's right. There are all these other things to do with time. It used to be people would wonder what the hell they were going to do for the winter. (Laughs) Then a big book would come out—a big, wonderful book—and everybody would be reading it to pass the time. It was a very primitive experiment, before television, where people would have to look at ink on paper, for God's sake. I myself grew up where radio was very important. I'd come home from school and turn on the radio. There were funny comedians and wonderful music and there were plays. I used to pass time with radio. Now, you don't have to be literate to have a nice time.

You've said that TV is one of the most viable art forms today.

Well, it is. It works like a dream. It's a way to hold attention, and it's awfully good at that. For a lot of people, TV is life itself. Churches used to provide people with better company than they had at home, but now no matter what your neighborhood life or family life is like, you turn on the television and you get relatives, family. I don't know if you've heard about this, but scientists have created baby geese who believe that an airplane is their mother. Human beings will believe in all kinds of things that aren't true, and that's okay. And TV is a part of that.

In your opinion, what's good on TV?

I have seen episodes of TV which would have been major Broadway plays in the '20s and '30s. That's where so much of our great writing is going on, if very rarely. "Law & Order", for example, deals with very subtle issues and social problems, very effectively and truthfully. That's one of the best things going, that show.

2007 has been dubbed the Year of Kurt Vonnegut. When we spoke a few years back, you said that the acceptance of your community has always been important to you. Is this paradise found?

Well, paradise lost, really. We all should have extended families. We need them, just like we need vitamins and minerals. And most of us don't have those extended families anymore. I had one in Indianapolis, when I was born, which was in 1922. I had uncles and aunts all over the place, and cousins, and family businesses that I could go into maybe, whole rows of cottages that were full of my relatives. There was always someone to talk with, to play with, to learn from. I've lost all of that. They have been disbursed.

But the community more generally speaking, is honoring you now—with celebrations and festivals. What do you make of that?

It's a very sweet honor. Of course, what it is, it's the idea of librarians there in Indianapolis—they have a great public library system, of which I was a great beneficiary when I was a kid—and it's a celebration of books and reading, really. Librarians, real heroes of our nation, have come forward to make this celebration, and that's a wonderful thing.

Is there another book in you, by chance?

No. Look, I'm 84 years old. Writers of fiction have usually

done their best work by the time they're 45. Chess masters are through when they're 35, and so are baseball players. There are plenty of other people writing. Let them do it.

So what's the old man's game, then?

My country is in ruins. So I'm a fish in a poisoned fish bowl. I'm mostly just heartsick about this. There should have been hope. This should have been a great country. But we are despised all over the world now. I was hoping to build a country and add to its literature. That's why I served in World War II, and that's why I wrote books.

When someone reads one of your books, what would you like them to take from the experience?

Well, I'd like the guy—or the girl, of course—to put the book down and think, "This is the greatest man who ever lived." (Laughs)

THE LAST
INTERVIEW

INTERVIEW BY HEATHER AUGUSTYN

FIRST PUBLISHED ONLINE AT *IN THESE TIMES*
MAY 9, 2007

On April 27, Kurt Vonnegut was scheduled to speak in In-
dianapolis as part of the city-proclaimed The Year of Vonnegut.
On February 28, in what was to be his last interview, I spoke
by phone with Vonnegut, who was home in New York.

We did not talk for long because he was not well, but we
discussed memories of family vacations, his ancestors and what
it means to be a family. Sadly, a member of our family is gone,
a member of our karass, a true American, and one hell of a
writer. The following is our conversation.

What about Indiana explains why you write, what you
write, and who you are?

Well, there was certainly plenty to write about. Indiana is a
very divided state, which creates a kind of electricity. During the Civil War, the governor sent the legislature home
because he was afraid southern Indiana would go with the
Confederacy. So that tension is really very exciting. Of
course, Indiana was strongly racist in some places. The last
lynching to take place north of the Mason-Dixon line was
in Marion in 1930, and when I was a kid, the headquarters
of the Ku Klux Klan was in my home town of Indianapolis.
But Indiana was also the home and birthplace of Eugene

Debs, the great American socialist. And so the ding-dong, back-and-forth was very entertaining. I was, of course, on the side of Debs.

Did that influence you when you were younger, and later the content of your novels?

In the public schools, I learned what America was supposed to be—you, you know, a beacon of liberty to the rest of the world. And obviously, that wasn't the case. I wrote a letter to Iraq, an open letter signed Uncle Sam [laughs], and what it said was: "Dear Iraq. Do like us. At the beginning of democracy, a bit of genocide and ethnic cleansing is quite okay. After a hundred years, you have to let your slaves go. And, after a hundred and fifty years, you have to let your women vote and hold public office." Some democracy. Anyway, when I was young, I noticed these contradictions and, of course, they were quite acceptable to a lot of people, but not to me.

Tell me a little bit about your childhood in Indiana. I know that you've written that you used to visit Lake Maxinkuckee.

Yeah, well, I've said in my speeches that everyone needs an extended family. The great American disease is loneliness. We no longer have extended family. But I had one. There were lots of Vonneguts in the phone book and my mother was a Lieber, and there were Liebers there too. And at Lake

Maxinkuckee there were a row of cottages, one of which we owned, and so I was surrounded by relatives all of the time. You know, cousins, uncles and aunts. It was heaven. And that has since been dispersed.

Do you think that might have had any part in your book *Cat's Cradle*?

I don't really trace the roots of any of my ideas. One basic attitude I've learned from my family is that they were free-thinkers. People stopped calling themselves that because it was so specifically German and the Germans were so hated during the First World War. And so, I am now honorary president of the American Humanist Association, which is just the very same thing.

But you know, I don't mock religion at all. It's very helpful to people. I had a particular war buddy named Bernie O'Hare and he was so disgusted that we bombed civilians, because he thought we were the good guys. He had thought we were careful not to hurt civilians and it was the Nazis, the bad guys, who didn't care what civilians they killed. Then we saw the Dresden Fire Bombing, when the cruise ship brought us home after the war and we parted company, I said, "What did you learn?" and he replied, "I'll never believe my government again."

Freethinkers. They're like humanists, in that they were influenced by science, not what was in the Old Testament.

I know a bit about them.

My ancestors on both sides of the family came over here about the time of the Civil War. One of them lost a leg and went back to Germany. Anyway, but they were all free-thinkers. They were educated. They weren't refugees at all. They were opportunists, looking to build things, businesses to go into.

Here is what my great grandfather Clemens Vonnegut said one time about Jesus, "If what he said was good, and it was marvelous, what did it matter if he was god or not?" And I am enormously influenced by the Sermon on the Mount. But I gotta go. I'm not well. Good luck.

Born November 11, 1922 in Indianapolis, Indiana, **KURT VONNEGUT'S** black humor, satiric voice, and incomparable imagination first captured America's attention in *The Sirens of Titan* in 1959 and established him as "a true artist" (*The New York Times*) with *Cat's Cradle* in 1963. He was, as Graham Greene declared, "one of the best living American writers." Vonnegut died on April 11, 2007.

CAROLE MALLORY is an American author, actress and former model who appeared in the films *Looking for Mr. Goodbar* and *The Stepford Wives*.

J. C. GABEL is the founding editor and publisher of *Stop Smiling* magazine. He edits and publishes Stop Smiling Books.

JOSEPH HELLER was born in Brooklyn in 1923. In 1961, he published *Catch-22*, which became a bestseller and, in 1970, a film. He went on to write such novels as *Good as Gold, God Knows, Picture This, Closing Time* (the sequel to *Catch-22*), and *Portrait of an Artist, as an Old Man.* Heller died in December 1999.

ROBERT K. MUSIL is a scholar-in-residence and adjunct professor in the School of International Studies at American University where he teaches in the Program on Global Environmental Politics and the Nuclear Studies Institute.

J. RENTILLY is a Los Angeles-based journalist who writes about film, music, literature, and pop culture for a variety of national and international publications.

HEATHER AUGUSTYN is a correspondent for *The Times of Northwest Indiana* and a contributing editor for *Shore Magazine*. She has written for *The Village Voice* and *E! The Environmental Magazine* and is an avid reader of Vonnegut's works.

THE LAST INTERVIEW SERIES

KURT VONNEGUT: THE LAST INTERVIEW

"I think it can be tremendously refreshing if a creator of literature has something on his mind other than the history of literature so far. Literature should not disappear up its own asshole, so to speak."

$15.95 / $17.95 CAN
978-1-61219-090-7
ebook: 978-1-61219-091-4

LEARNING TO LIVE FINALLY: THE LAST INTERVIEW
JACQUES DERRIDA

"I am at war with myself, it's true, you couldn't possibly know to what extent ... I say contradictory things that are, we might say, in real tension; they are what construct me, make me live, and will make me die."

translated by PASCAL-ANNE BRAULT and MICHAEL NAAS

$15.95 / $17.95 CAN
978-1-61219-094-5
ebook: 978-1-61219-032-7

ROBERTO BOLAÑO: THE LAST INTERVIEW

"Posthumous: It sounds like the name of a Roman gladiator, an unconquered gladiator. At least that's what poor Posthumous would like to believe. It gives him courage."

translated by SYBIL PEREZ and others

$15.95 / $17.95 CAN
978-1-61219-095-2
ebook: 978-1-61219-033-4